Running a
Public
Relations
Department

PR IN PRACTICE SERIES

Running a Public Relations Department

Mike Beard

Second Edition

the Institute *of* Public Relations

KOGAN PAGE

First published in 1997
Reprinted in 2000
Second edition published in 2001

Kogan Page Limited
120 Pentonville Road
London N1 9JN

British Library Cataloguing in Publication Data

A CIP record for this book is available from the British Library.

ISBN 0 7494 3424 4

Typeset by Jean Cussons Typesetting, Diss, Norfolk
Printed and bound in Great Britain by Biddles Ltd, Guildford and King's Lynn

Contents

About the author

Mike Beard, FIPR, is Director of Communication and Marketing at Wastepack Group, the fast growing environmental services company. He has occupied the post of corporate communication director in major international companies, including Taylor Woodrow and Lucas Industries. He has held responsibility for programmes covering all audiences including investor relations, marketing communication, internal communication and government relations. He also has experience in consultancy including two years as Managing Director of Burson-Marsteller Singapore. Mike is a former chairman of the International Committee of the UK Institute of Public Relations, was Honorary Treasurer of the Institute in 1992 and served as President in 1994. He is a holder of the CERP in-house practitioner prize.

Foreword

Life as a public relations practitioner is usually frantic! Always too much to do and to very tight deadlines. However, a well-structured environment, with good working practices and staff who are trained to deal with the essential mundanities as well as the high-level work, makes life much smoother, even fun.

The public relations manager should be forward thinking, skilled in the practice of public relations, a good manager – of people and resources and proficient at administration. Of course they may have assistance, that's the essence of team work, but there is absolutely no excuse for sloppiness or disinterest in any aspect of work.

Many consultancies have got to grips with these issues and there are dozens of efficient in-house departments. However, there is very little advice and guidance about how to manage either consultancies or in-house departments in an effective manner.

This book, written by Mike Beard, tackles the topic of running an in-house department with sense and energy. With a wealth of experience of managing large departments, Mike approaches the subject systematically and logically. He starts with the various types of organisation and their respective needs. He then looks briefly at the areas of activity covered by public relations and at the range of techniques employed. Mike then examines in detail departmental planning, managing budgets and delivering value for money. People are at the core of the business and a substantial part of the book focuses on creating and managing a team and managing internal and external relationships. There are then some very useful and practical sections on creating a public relations manual, general administration and working with consultancies.

Finally, Mike turns to the personal development of the public relations manager. Career development and the vitally important area of ethical standards bring the book to a suitable and powerful conclusion. This book is a comprehensive guide to setting up and managing an in-house department and provides a solid foundation from which to build professional and effective public relations practice.

Anne Gregory, Series Editor

PR in Practice Series

Published in association with the Institute of Public Relations
Series Editor: Anne Gregory

Kogan Page has joined forces with the Institute of Public Relations to publish this unique series which is designed specifically to meet the needs of the increasing numbers of people seeking to enter the public relations profession and the large band of existing PR professionals. Taking a practical, action-oriented approach, the books in the series concentrate on the day-to-day issues of public relations practice and management rather than academic history. They provide ideal primers for all those on IPR, CAM and CIM courses or those taking NVQs in PR. For PR practitioners, they provide useful refreshers and ensure that their knowledge and skills are kept up to date.

Anne Gregory is one of the UK's leading public relations academies. She is Head of the School of Business Strategy and Assistant Dean of Leeds Business School, a faculty of Leeds Metropolitan University. Before becoming an academic, Anne spent 12 years in public relations practice and has experience at a senior level both in-house and in consultancy. She remains involved in consultancy work and is a non-executive director of Bradford Community Health Trust with special responsibility for communication issues. Anne is Consultant Editor of the PR in Practice series and is the editor of *Public Relations in Practice*, also in this series.

Other titles in the series:

Creativity in Public Relations by Andy Green
Effective Media Relations by Michael Bland, Alison Theaker and David Wragg
Effective Writing Skills for Public Relations by John Foster
Managing Activism by Denise Deegan
Planning and Managing Public Relations Campaigns by Anne Gregory
Public Relations: A practical guide to the basics by Philip Henslowe
Public Relations in Practice edited by Anne Gregory
Risk Issues and Crisis Management in Public Relations by Michael Regester
    and Judy Larkin

Forthcoming titles:

Online Public Relations by David Phillips
Strategic Public Relations by Sandra Oliver

The above titles are available from all good bookshops. To obtain further information, please contact the publishers at the address below:

Kogan Page Ltd
120 Pentonville Road
London N1 9JN
Tel: 020 7278 0433   Fax: 020 7837 6348
www.kogan-page.co.uk

1

Managing for reputation

GOOD MANAGEMENT WINS ALLIES

Public relations is defined by the Institute of Public Relations (IPR) as 'the discipline which looks after reputation'. The aim of this book is to help practitioners manage this function in a way which is productive and cost effective and which will enhance the reputation of the department internally and externally.

A public relations department which is well managed will win respect internally and gain allies who will help it to achieve its aims. A department which is well regarded externally will be trusted and consulted and be an asset to the company.

Of course, these principles are equally true of any other activity but they are particularly relevant for public relations practitioners because of the history and perceptions of the function. It is necessary to take account of these factors to understand the reasons why good management practice matters so much in successful public relations.

A NEW MANAGEMENT DISCIPLINE

Perhaps most significant is the fact that public relations is a relatively new management discipline in its organised and developed form. There have always been natural communicators and the pioneers of organised public relations began to appear in the 1920s. However, the planned and sustained application of communication techniques with the aim of influencing opinion and behaviour only started to become standard management practice in the 1950s and 1960s. Because of this and as a result of the rapid growth of the profession, the average age of practitioners is relatively low.

Many people working in public relations do not have a formal qualification in the discipline. The IPR has supported and promoted its own public relations diploma for many years. However, it was not until the early 1990s that the IRP began formally to recognise a number of first degrees and postgraduate diplomas as covering the necessary educational matrix.

The shortage of qualified practitioners has been accompanied by a lack of general management expertise in the function. This is because the business schools have been slow to include public relations within the management education and development curriculum. So, we have a young discipline, sparsely qualified, often reporting to general managers with a low understanding of the role of PR. The resultant expectations can be low. In these circumstances high-quality management performance will push public relations way up the corporate agenda.

There are other environmental factors which create pressure on public relations to perform. Some management colleagues may have a poor view of the function. This can be based on a total lack of understanding of the scope and capability of the activity. It can result from prejudice based on abuse of the terminology such as the dreaded 'just a public relations exercise' beloved of the media.

It does not help that sales promotion assistants offering visits to facilities from time share to hotel dining rooms often describe their work as public relations. The problem is compounded by the fact that events management is often within the responsibility of the public relations officer, thus stimulating the 'gin and tonic' image, now thankfully fast fading. The idea that 'getting on well with people' is the major qualification for working in public relations is another myth which may yet take decades to disappear.

A world of 'experts'

Without depressing ourselves too much, we also need to remember that many of our colleagues consider themselves much more expert at our function than they are in other fields such as finance or information technology. After all, how many general managers will admit to being poor or indifferent personal communicators? Many people believe they have a natural ability to write crisp and interesting copy and to select a stunning creative concept.

Taking these points into account, the public relations manager must get the organisation to assess and manage its reputation through its behaviour and its communication. The manager must also win the budgets that are necessary to carry out the agreed programmes.

Good management of the public relations function will make the difference between the success or failure of this task and it will help to give the public relations manager an equal status with other key management disciplines within the organisation.

THE EFFECT OF ORGANISATIONAL ENVIRONMENT

The management style of the department will be influenced substantially by the nature, structure and culture of the organisation within which it operates.

Public relations within a business environment will require a different approach and balance of skills from that which might be required in the public sector or within a voluntary organisation. Within the business sector there will be great differences between industries. A company in the consumer area will not have the same style or requirements as an enterprise selling its products or services on a business-to-business basis.

Operating in a highly regulated area such as financial or professional services or in a utility will create its own special needs. A long-established company in a traditional field is likely to have much more defined ways of doing things than a relatively young organisation in information technology or the leisure industry.

Some businesses have formal and highly structured ways of doing things and this is likely to be the case in the public sector.

The use of planned public relations in the public sector is a relatively recent phenomenon and there may be more barriers for the public relations manager to break down than in the commercial world.

The voluntary sector can vary enormously. Working for a charity can be great fun and highly informal, while a professional body might be more staid. In either case it might be necessary to clear decisions through a complex structure of voluntary committee members.

No two organisations are the same

We must avoid generalisations for there are lively and progressive merchant banks and professional bodies, just as there are dull fashion houses and charities. No two organisations are the same. This should not matter to the modern public relations manager who possesses well-developed transferable skills. But it will influence the structure and style of the department.

The most important trait for a successful public relations practitioner is sensitivity – that is, the ability to understand the feelings and reactions of a diversity of audiences. This trait will be of great benefit as you set out your departmental stall within your own organisation.

MANAGING AT DIFFERENT LEVELS

Public relations departments can operate at a variety of levels and where you sit in the organisation will have a significant effect on the workload and the way you organise. Figure 1.1 shows typical reporting structures for PR departments.

In a large operation the central or corporate department sets the standards for public relations and will have to take a broad overview of all activities. It may control directly the work of subsidiary or regional public relations officers. Alternatively, the officers may report to local general managers with a 'dotted line' to corporate public relations. Either way there has to be a coordinated approach to communication to ensure that a consistent message about the organisation is presented.

In corporate departments PR officers report to the senior managers of the organisation who are under pressure to produce

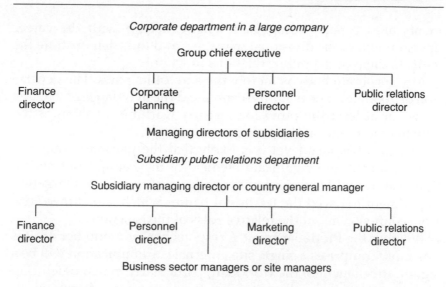

Figure 1.1 *Typical reporting structures for public relations departments*

results. In turn this leads to extra pressure to perform for the public relations professionals. Often the senior managers, such as leaders of public companies, are of mature age and prefer to take their advice from practitioners of comparable age. This means that it will be necessary to have a more mature balance of practitioners than might be necessary in, say, the product promotional area of a consumer business.

Corporate departments also require a wider balance of skills than subsidiaries. Usually these include such areas as government relations, speech writing and investor relations in the case of public companies. Language skills can be vital in an organisation with an international spread.

Operating at subsidiary level

The public relations department at subsidiary, company, divisional or regional level will have to satisfy the requirements of the local operating management as well as meeting any criteria imposed from the centre.

The PR department can play a unique role in uniting the division with the corporate centre. By representing to the centre the interests of the division it can make sure that the local achievements are properly recognised. This can help with the career development of the divisional managers and thus demonstrate the value to them of the public relations function!

Any corporate body is merely the sum of its parts. The generation of good news pegs for the centre and the avoidance of 'banana skins', or at least the provision of early warnings of them, is the way to win friends at head office.

At this subsidiary level it is likely that the particular range of tasks will call for a significant element of marketing communication skill. It will be necessary to work closely with the marketing department to avoid the territorial battles which sometimes arise from confusion about the relative roles of the functions.

Whether the PR department is responsible for a number of sites or simply comprises a single site, internal communication will be a significant element of the workload, particularly in manufacturing and other activities which involve large numbers of employees. You will also have to manage local community relations, particularly for the site team in a business which creates nuisance for its neighbours.

THE INTERNATIONAL CHALLENGE

One of the most challenging places to manage public relations is in an overseas subsidiary or representative office. You will be one of the key participants in ensuring that corporate messages are not corrupted but nevertheless presented in a way which will enable them to be understood locally. Conversely, you will also need to explain the quirks of the local culture to the overseas principals.

In any of these roles you could be the only public relations professional, with no colleagues to give support and encouragement. In this situation it is just as important as ever to ensure that you manage yourself well. You should establish proper plans and budgets for your activities, and monitor and report on their progress. This will prepare you for the bigger tasks in your future career and will enhance your status and achievement in your current role.

2

Areas of activity

PUBLIC RELATIONS DEFINED

The IPR sees public relations as synonymous with reputation – it is the result of what you do, what you say and what others say about you. The IPR goes on to define public relations practice as the discipline which looks after reputation with the aim of earning understanding and support, and influencing opinion and behaviour.

Although an organisation must have a consistent approach to communication and reputation management, the overall process can be conveniently divided into a number of areas. The terminology and divisions are not universally agreed and consistent, but most practitioners look at the discipline in several main sectors comprising:

- financial and corporate communication;
- government affairs;
- marketing communication;
- internal communication;
- community relations.

Each of these sectors has distinct characteristics which will affect the structure and management of the public relations department. The span of your responsibility will therefore significantly influence the special skills and the size and type of resource you need, defining your management approach.

We are not attempting to provide guidance on the planning of public relations programmes but simply to outline some of the specific characteristics of each main sector which will impact upon departmental management. In each case you need to look at:

● the purpose of the activity;
● the target 'publics' or audiences;
● typical programme content;
● the principal interfaces;
● any specialist skills and experience required.

Table 2.1 summarises these areas and planning factors.

Table 2.1 *Management planning matrix*

Public relations areas	Planning factors
financial and corporate	purpose
government affairs	audiences
marketing communication	programme content
internal communication	working partnerships
community relations	skills needed

FINANCIAL COMMUNICATION

Purpose

This is mainly a concern for public companies although it is also important for other organisations which require borrowings or may wish to float publicly at some future date. One major purpose of a financial communication programme is to enable companies to raise equity on favourable terms, to resist hostile bids, and to facilitate acquisitions through a strong share price. Just as important is the ability to borrow on favourable terms as a result of a good debt rating. The financial community is also important because of its ability to bring deals to a company which it knows and regards, and because of the community's important general role in forming opinion towards companies. (See Figure 2.1.)

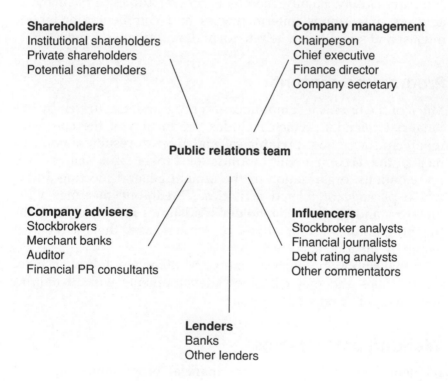

Shareholders
Institutional shareholders
Private shareholders
Potential shareholders

Company management
Chairperson
Chief executive
Finance director
Company secretary

Public relations team

Company advisers
Stockbrokers
Merchant banks
Auditor
Financial PR consultants

Influencers
Stockbroker analysts
Financial journalists
Debt rating analysts
Other commentators

Lenders
Banks
Other lenders

Figure 2.1 *Financial communication interfaces for the public relations department*

Audiences

The principal target audiences include existing and potential institutional shareholders. The role of private shareholders is much less significant but cannot be ignored, especially since pressure groups are increasingly using this route for gaining a voice in companies. The broker analysts who publish research for investors have a key role in any financial communication programme. The banks and other lenders who may subscribe to various forms of debt utilised by the company can be just as important as investors. The debt-rating agencies are of considerable significance. The role of financial journalists has also to be given great weight for they can influence vital audiences who are not themselves following the company closely. Finally, there is a general audience of financial advisers, institutions, intermediaries and commentators whose interest and support can help to form the company's reputation.

Programme content

Much of the financial communication programme is driven by the 'financial calendar' which includes production of the company report and accounts, preliminary and interim results announcements, the accompanying rounds of broker and shareholder presentations, organisation of the annual general meeting and a whole package of related activities. One-to-one meetings with investors and private shareholder roadshows may also figure in the programme. Presentations to lenders and the media also feature in the total approach.

Special situations such as mergers, defended takeover bids, rights issues and major business developments will all require specialist public relations support.

Working partnerships

In planning and implementing financial programmes you will need to work closely with colleagues in the finance and company secretarial functions. There will be a continual exposure to the most senior members of the board. It will also be necessary to work closely with the company's advisers such as company stockbrokers, auditors, merchant banks and financial public relations consultants.

Skills needed

Financial communication is perhaps the most demanding area of public relations management, requiring meticulous attention to detail and a finely developed judgement. Practitioners must have a good working knowledge of the listing requirements and takeover codes of the stock exchanges on which the company has a listing and of all other statutory requirements and relevant codes of practice. A basic understanding of company accounts is vital. Practical skill and experience in speech writing and presentation production, publication production and financial media relations are essential additions to the general public relations abilities that are needed. The practitioner must be comfortable in working with senior company management and specialist external advisers.

GOVERNMENT AFFAIRS

Purpose

In some organisations this area of activity is referred to as 'public affairs', a term otherwise used as an alternative generic for 'public relations'. The purpose of the activity is to ensure that governments and other public bodies are aware of the organisation and take account of its legitimate interests in framing public policy, legislation and regulation. In turn, the organisation is aware of future legislative ideas and can attempt to influence these and also plan its own future strategies accordingly. In addition, a broad knowledge of public policy can enable the organisation to be a better corporate citizen.

For many bodies there are additional relationships with government, perhaps as an important customer or as a provider of funding to the voluntary sector. In these situations the commercial or funding relationship is usually handled separately, perhaps by the sales and marketing department or the fund-raising specialist. Sometimes the roles are indistinguishable, such as when lobbying for a major defence contract or for the funding of a new arts project.

Audiences

The principal target audiences include elected representatives and public officials at all levels of government, as well as intergovernmental bodies such as the European Union or the Association of

11

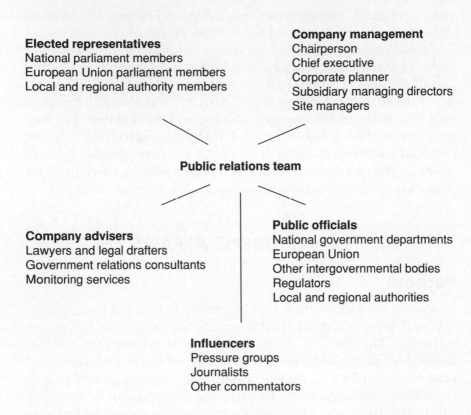

Elected representatives
National parliament members
European Union parliament members
Local and regional authority members

Company management
Chairperson
Chief executive
Corporate planner
Subsidiary managing directors
Site managers

Public relations team

Company advisers
Lawyers and legal drafters
Government relations consultants
Monitoring services

Public officials
National government departments
European Union
Other intergovernmental bodies
Regulators
Local and regional authorities

Influencers
Pressure groups
Journalists
Other commentators

Figure 2.2 *Government affairs interfaces for the public relations department*

South East Asian Nations. National governments are obviously of major importance. State, regional and local government relations also have to be managed. (See Figure 2.2.)

The relationships between different levels of government become increasingly complex. For example, much legislation that goes before the UK Parliament is now initiated in the European Union, although there can be flexibility about the method of national implementation. The situation is further complicated by the devolution of power to bodies such as the Scottish Parliament and the London Mayor and Assembly.

Public bodies and agencies, from the United Nations to national and local statutory bodies, all have their own importance. A contractor bidding for a school extension may have to satisfy the school governors that the work will be carried out in a sympathetic way. Although public sector business is usually awarded on a tender basis, it may well be necessary to establish a suitable reputation in order to pre-qualify.

Programme content

Programmes in public affairs include a major element of research and monitoring of parliamentary reports and similar sources. The production of clear and well-argued position papers and the arrangement of briefing meetings are likely to dominate the lobbying process. When dealing with specific issues there may come a time when it is necessary to enlist extensive specialist support or public opinion. At this point a broad range of public relations activities may be required. At all times there will be a need to carry out routine contact programmes with relevant individuals so that they have familiarity with and are favourably disposed towards your employer when help is needed.

Working partnerships

In the government affairs arena you will need to work with specialist monitoring services and utilise specialist advisers with a close knowledge of the political and parliamentary processes in the countries which are of importance to you. At some point there may be an involvement with lawyers and parliamentary draftspeople.

Skills needed

The skills you will need include a working knowledge of the processes of government and a sensitivity to the political complexities faced by the people you seek to influence. In particular there must be a keen awareness of when public pressure is likely to help and when it will be counterproductive. Technical skills required include the ability to draft short, well-argued position papers.

MARKETING COMMUNICATION

Purpose

Few business subjects have had as much debate over the years as the difference between marketing and public relations. A short paper written for the IPR by Carol Friend of Pielle may clarify the issue for general managers. The paper quotes the Chartered Institute of Marketing definition of marketing as the management process responsible for identifying, anticipating and satisfying customers' requirements, profitably. It goes on to explain that the reputation of an organisation, business or brand impacts on its marketing. Public relations helps to provide the appropriate reputation environment in which professional marketing can take place. In addition, the broad range of techniques that public relations employs makes a valuable contribution to the total marketing mix. Public relations makes an equally valuable contribution to other functions of an organisation as described here and so is not a subset of marketing. (See Figure 2.3.)

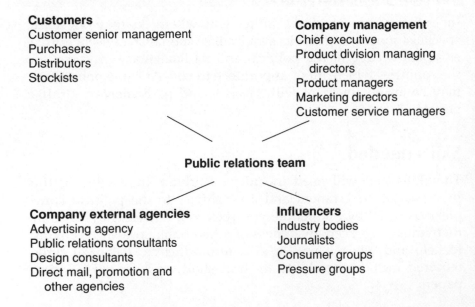

Customers
Customer senior management
Purchasers
Distributors
Stockists

Company management
Chief executive
Product division managing
   directors
Product managers
Marketing directors
Customer service managers

Public relations team

Company external agencies
Advertising agency
Public relations consultants
Design consultants
Direct mail, promotion and
   other agencies

Influencers
Industry bodies
Journalists
Consumer groups
Pressure groups

Figure 2.3 *Marketing communication intrfaces for the public relations department*

Just as corporate reputation is vitally important when customers choose their suppliers of products and services, so the public relations practitioner plays an important role in sales and marketing. Senior management of potential clients are an appropriate audience for corporate public relations programmes. The person targeted by the sales and marketing team may have to get the decision to purchase approved at board level.

Beyond this, the public relations manager may have a direct responsibility for marketing or at least for carrying out those marketing support activities which rely on techniques which are also used in public relations, such as media relations and sponsorship. There is the potential for territorial conflict in some organisations, so you will need to be alert to the implications of this.

Major differences usually exist between the structures adopted by companies marketing consumer goods and those which sell 'business to business'. In the former there will usually be a large marketing department and there may well be public relations officers and consultancies working on marketing communication and reporting to marketing managers. Here lies the greatest potential for misunderstanding and a need for good teamwork with the corporate public relations activity.

Audiences

Customers are, of course, the prime audience for marketing communication. In a voluntary body they could be potential donors or helpers. The potential customer base for a soft drinks company could include most of the population, while the producer of a missile system might have only a handful of governmental customers. Other target audiences may include distributors and stockists. Industry bodies and regulators may be important along with a variety of commentators and opinion formers. When marketing to businesses and other organisations, the decision-making process can be influenced at a variety of levels.

Programme content

The programmes used in marketing communication, particularly in highly competitive consumer areas, often depend on a high degree of creativity. A wide range of techniques is used, including:

media relations; events management and promotions; sponsorship; loyalty clubs and affinity schemes; demonstrations; exhibitions and conferences.

Working partnerships

The public relations manager will need to work closely with marketing colleagues and with product or general managers. Large budgets may be deployed and a wide range of external agencies used, including advertising agencies, design consultancies, and direct mail and promotional specialists. The public relations team will need to work hard to make it understood that they are able to contribute more than the 'free editorial publicity' which some colleagues will see as their main role.

Skills needed

A wide range of public relations skills is likely to be required by the public relations team working in the marketing communication area. In many areas such as health care or professional and financial services a specialist knowledge of the regulatory environment will be most important. In many sectors it will be important to have the aptitude for conceiving highly creative solutions to communication tasks. A knowledge of creative brainstorming techniques will be invaluable.

INTERNAL COMMUNICATION

Purpose

Internal communication is concerned with the relationships between an organisation and its employees. Similar management procedures can be applied to communication with the members or volunteers within, say, a professional body or a charitable organisation. A major aim is to facilitate the recruitment and retention of high-quality employees who will make a positive contribution to the organisation's activities. Another is to ensure that the workforce is well informed so that performance and job satisfaction can be maximised. A sense of involvement and belonging makes for a happier and more successful working environment. (See Figure 2.4.)

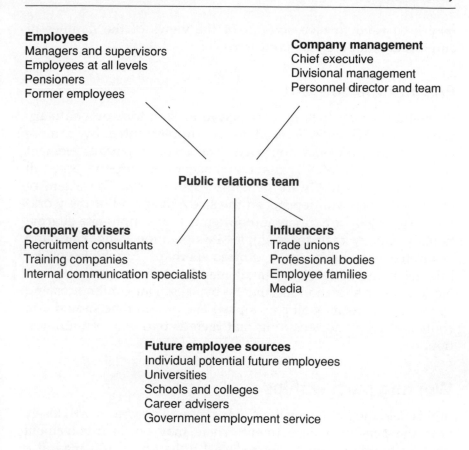

Employees
Managers and supervisors
Employees at all levels
Pensioners
Former employees

Company management
Chief executive
Divisional management
Personnel director and team

Public relations team

Company advisers
Recruitment consultants
Training companies
Internal communication specialists

Influencers
Trade unions
Professional bodies
Employee families
Media

Future employee sources
Individual potential future employees
Universities
Schools and colleges
Career advisers
Government employment service

Figure 2.4 *Internal communication interfaces for the public relations department*

Audiences

The main audience is obviously current employees at all levels, including management, and in all the locations. Potential employees are also significant so that the highest-quality recruits can be found to support expansion and fill vacancies. Many opinion formers may also be targeted. These might include university staff, careers advisers, recruitment consultants and other specialists. The government department of employment is another potential influence in areas where there is competition for employees. Formal and informal relationships may also occur with trade unions and professional bodies. In some situations there may be a need to take account of the views of the families of employees and potential employees.

Programme content

Programmes may include a structure of statutory or voluntary consultation which will need to be supplemented by a more personal and informal approach. The most important element should be team briefing, based on managers and supervisors at all levels talking regularly to their immediate teams. The extent of other initiatives will depend on the size and spread of the workforce. There will be a different requirement for a multi-site international company than for a single-site operation. Magazines and newsletters are likely to be utilised, perhaps supplemented by briefing notes. Video and e-mail may have an important place. Noticeboards, site announcements, management conferences and factory meetings may all play a part. The programme should also contain elements for ensuring that there is two-way communication.

Working partnerships

In this field the public relations manager will need to work closely with the personnel department. There may be an involvement with trade unions and other external influencers. You may also need to work with external training companies, recruitment advisers and internal communication consultants. Interface with managers throughout the organisation will be vital, for staff departments can only facilitate internal communication. The responsibility rests with the line managers.

Skills needed

You will need to understand the legal implications of and requirements for communication in your organisation. An extreme sensitivity to different levels of interest in messages is required. Apart from a wide range of public relations skills you are likely to need periodical publication design and production experience. The ability to translate management information into clear and simple briefing notes will perhaps be the most important attribute.

OTHER CORPORATE AUDIENCES

Purpose

The reputation of any organisation can be affected by the opinions of a variety of corporate audiences, which have differing degrees of direct relationship but are in contact with the same prime audiences. In addition, the attitude of suppliers can be crucial to organisational performance, particularly in sectors such a retailing and manufacturing. (See Figure 2.5.)

The corporate aim is to be understood and respected by the more general audiences and to be a preferred customer to your suppliers. This will mean that your key publics are hearing positive comments which enhance your reputation and that the performance of your suppliers gives you a competitive advantage.

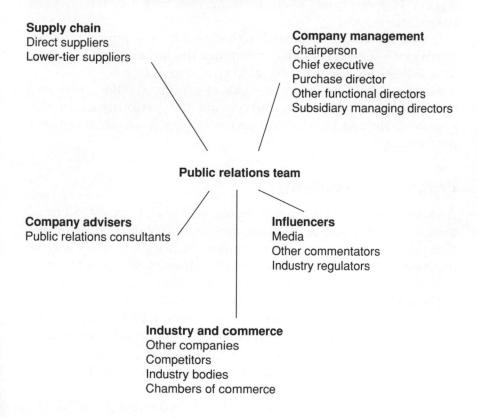

Supply chain
Direct suppliers
Lower-tier suppliers

Company management
Chairperson
Chief executive
Purchase director
Other functional directors
Subsidiary managing directors

Public relations team

Company advisers
Public relations consultants

Influencers
Media
Other commentators
Industry regulators

Industry and commerce
Other companies
Competitors
Industry bodies
Chambers of commerce

Figure 2.5   *Other corporate interfaces for the public relations department*

Audiences

The target audiences include other organisations of a similar status, such as the other government departments if you are working in a ministry, or other major companies if you are employed by a large business.

Industry bodies such as the Confederation of British Industry and chambers of commerce are important to a business organisation. If you are employed by one professional body such as the Institute of Public Relations, the opinions of other bodies such as the accountants or the personnel practitioners can be influential.

The views of competitors should not be neglected. If your common audiences can see that they respect you this will enhance your own standing greatly. Another factor is that competitors who respect you are more likely to treat you with caution in your shared marketplace.

If you work in a regulated activity such as a public utility, a charity or a financial services company, the attitude of the regulatory authorities might be crucial to your success.

Most entities rely upon a network of suppliers, who in turn will have their own suppliers. Influencing the performance of this supply chain can be a critical factor in your own organisation's performance.

Programme content

A major element in your programmes will be the fact that all these audiences will share or overhear the communication programmes that you direct at more specific audiences. Your suppliers may be exposed to the same media as your customers. Other companies will see the advertising you direct at the financial community.

Depending on the needs of your organisation, this may be enough. Sometimes some of these groups will be targeted by programmes developed at subsidiary level. In any event, their senior management will certainly be exposed to many of your corporate communication programmes and you will need to consider this in your planning.

It can be useful to maintain direct and cordial but guarded relationships with your competitors, perhaps to exchange formally your various public documents and statements. There will be some external issues where you wish to adopt a common approach with your competitors in the best interests of your sector.

It may be wise to extend the mailing of your company magazine or report and accounts to some of the groups discussed here. It can be valuable for you and your management colleagues to play an active part in the relevant industry bodies.

There should be regular communication with suppliers to help them to understand your business and to feel part of your team. This may be handled at subsidiary level, but you might add an additional process where your chief executive meets large suppliers at a senior level once or twice a year.

It is difficult to generalise about the best way to communicate with regulatory authorities as no two sectors are the same. Certainly, you should be as open as possible, avoid excessive entertaining and deal with regulators professionally and with a friendly respect.

Working partnerships

In this area you are certain to be working closely with your senior management and with functional colleagues according to the organisational structure. For example, the purchasing director will be closely involved in supplier communication. If you are using a general public relations consultancy, the programmes they implement for you will impact these groups.

Skills needed

In this area you will need to deploy a range of general public relations skills, with specialist techniques to support any specific programmes you introduce. A degree of worldliness is necessary in order to anticipate and plan for the interest and reaction of these groups. This should extend to a fine judgement in designing your more targeted programmes so as to extend their reach and yet keep them cost effective.

COMMUNITY RELATIONS

Purpose

The categories described above cover the major stakeholders in the organisation, but of course there are many other publics who may be significant or who may consider that they have a legitimate interest in your employer's activities (see Figure 2.6). It is the burden of general public relations work with fringe audiences which is often least understood or valued by general management who, with some justification, may not see the point of it.

The aim of community relations or general public relations work can best be defined as the achievement of a good understanding and positive reputation with general audiences which have an interest in the organisation. Such an achievement is likely to be constrained by a lack of time and cash unless you work for a wealthy and altruistic organisation.

Audiences

The audience profile will include both local and national bodies, as well as international groups if you are operating in a number of countries.

The communities which live around your operations are one obvious audience and can be particularly important if you have a noisy factory or smelly production process. Students and school-children seeking help with projects can be a source of many enquiries. Pressure groups on a wide variety of issues, some relevant to your employer and many not, will seek information or your endorsement. Every business receives many requests for support from charities and good causes. Overall, it is impossible to list all the many diverse approaches you will have to handle from a variety of individuals and organisations.

Programme content

There will be differing approaches to managing public relations programmes for the variety of audiences discussed here. In some cases you will be communicating proactively and in others you will be responding to approaches.

For example, neighbourhood communities may be an important target and warrant a comprehensive programme, including newsletters, media relations, events and sponsorship. Other groups may be dealt with by utilising standard information packs that are targeted, for example, at schoolchildren or undergraduates. Pressure groups on subjects of prime importance are likely to

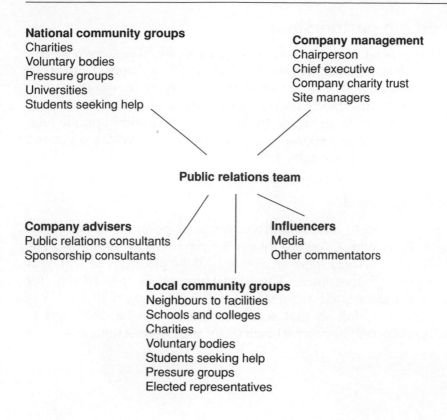

National community groups
Charities
Voluntary bodies
Pressure groups
Universities
Students seeking help

Company management
Chairperson
Chief executive
Company charity trust
Site managers

Public relations team

Company advisers
Public relations consultants
Sponsorship consultants

Influencers
Media
Other commentators

Local community groups
Neighbours to facilities
Schools and colleges
Charities
Voluntary bodies
Students seeking help
Pressure groups
Elected representatives

Figure 2.6 *Community relations interfaces for the public relations department*

be handled through a comprehensive issues management programme.

Many companies establish a charitable trust or appeals committee to deal with requests for donations. Certainly this whole area covers a miscellany of communication tasks and it is likely that demand will substantially outstrip the ability of the public relations department to resource them satisfactorily.

In many organisations the telephonists have become adept at directing calls to public relations when they have any doubt about how to handle them. This is quite natural but can be burdensome when they are added to the hundreds of unsolicited calls selling advertising space, seeking donations, offering myriad services or wanting to know the name of the chairperson's spouse.

Working partnerships

In this general area of public relations you are likely to work with many internal colleagues across a variety of functions. General or site managers will have a role in community relations. There will be a need to interface with personnel functions and those responsible for charitable giving if this is not handled within public relations. You may use sponsorship consultants or involve a general public relations consultancy.

Skills needed

You will need to deploy a broad range of public relations skills, particularly where you are managing proactive programmes. The ability to exercise judgement as to where the priorities lie will be of paramount importance. The development of procedures for dealing with related requests in a standard way will be a key management skill so that scarce resources can be dedicated to areas which will have a real benefit for the organisation.

3

Project management techniques

The programmes that you manage will contain a number of distinct elements that have particular management implications for you and your team. There are basic elements, such as media relations and briefing meetings, that will be included within your core public relations programme. From time to time, you will also have to manage major projects with specific purposes, which require substantial resources and involve several elements.

This chapter covers the general project management techniques that you can apply throughout your programme. Media relations, which will often be an important factor, is covered in Chapter 12.

MANAGING MAJOR PROJECTS

The activities that fall into this category include events such as a significant sponsorship, a company centenary celebration, a new product launch or a company merger.

You may be asked to manage a major project that has been initiated at board level or you may be its originator within your own programme. In either case, the way you manage the project can have a significant effect on your own reputation and that of your department.

When you are seeking approval for a large project, you need to prepare a formal proposal to submit to your management. You might start with an outline proposal document to avoid wasting effort developing detailed implementation plans that may not be needed. Your proposal should describe the project, its purpose and the benefits it will bring to your organisation. You should also be specific about the resources it will require, including internal and external costs. Include a statement of how the success of the project will be evaluated and judged. Sometimes you may need to present the proposal formally to your general management committee or board, so be prepared for this.

Once the project is approved, a more detailed action plan and timetable must be developed. This can be in a similar format to the action plan monitor described in Chapter 5. You should seek every opportunity to involve other departments in the implementation team in order to maximise your resources and widen the impact of your activity. You will also need to involve any external service suppliers as soon as possible so that budgets can be established and necessary facilities and capacity reserved.

From the outset, you should put a base programme of project review meetings in the diary, covering the whole period of the activity including the evaluation after the event. This will ensure that the key people involved are available, function as a cohesive team and that progress is monitored efficiently. You or a nominee should convene the meetings and one member of the team should update and issue the action monitor each time, together with any other brief notes from the meeting.

After your post-event evaluation meeting, a report should be prepared and circulated to management and all participants, demonstrating the success of the project in relation to the criteria established in advance and highlighting the lessons learnt during the process. This report should also be included in a master file for future reference, together with all the key documents and other material from the project.

MANAGING SMALLER PROJECTS

A simpler version of the process described above can be applied to smaller projects within your programmes. You may be producing a new corporate advertisement or updating your corporate brochure. Necessary actions, responsibility, costs, timetables, supplier information and other important aspects should be covered on a readily accessible project sheet.

This will be invaluable the next time a similar activity is required. It will also avoid a great deal of aggravation if the person responsible is taken ill or the activity needs to be repeated in an emergency.

In managing individual elements within your programmes you should consider the 'matrix' approach to planning and production described in Chapter 7.

WORKING WITH YOUR SUPPLIERS

You will need to work with a variety of external service suppliers including advertising and design agencies, research companies, audiovisual producers, Web site specialists and photographers. Relationships with public relations consultancies are dealt with in Chapter 14. A network of supportive suppliers will be of great benefit to you in delivering your programmes to a high standard, on time and within budget.

If you have a lot of money to spend, suppliers will be keen to have your business. The same will apply if you have a relatively small budget but work for an organisation that will add a prestige name to your supplier's lists (although your work may not be handled by the leading account teams). More typically, the challenge you have is to find smaller suppliers who will do just as good a job for you as the big names would. If this is the case, you should look for a high level of service and reliability at an affordable price. You want your business to be important to the supplier, but it is probably better for the relationship if it is not crucial to their survival. It is best to avoid any creative supplier staffed by prima donnas who will be averse to working within your own constraints.

Some of the principles for selecting a public relations consultancy described in Chapter 14 can be applied in these areas. You can identify potential suppliers by personal recommendation, by the evidence of the work you see, by looking within your own community, by working through industry bodies, by looking at media coverage or even by responding to the cold sales calls you receive. One important difference is that there is rarely any need for you to consider a retainer relationship – not even for an advertising agency. You can build a long-term relationship step by step, based on project-by-project performance.

Normally, you will be contracting with your suppliers, using your employer's purchase order system for a particular project based on their costed response to your brief. You should make it clear that the price you agree is the price you will pay and that any extras must be agreed in writing. It is worth making it clear that you expect your supplier to tell you clearly if anything you ask for during the project is outside the agreed budget and will create an extra cost. With a new supplier it is worthwhile to ask specifically and in writing if there is anything necessary to complete the job that is excluded from the price quoted.

BRIEFING SUPPLIERS

The quality of the briefs you give to your suppliers will largely determine the quality of the response you receive. This applies particularly when you are working with a supplier for the first time. Even when you have established a close-working relationship, you should still provide a written brief for every project – however small.

The brief should start with background information on the company and include any existing material that is relevant (unless you feel that the current material might set the designer off down the wrong track). If you decide this is not appropriate, you can always provide an explanation as to why the current material is no longer relevant.

You need to describe the item you require, explain its purpose and describe the target audience at which it is aimed. A communication aimed at finance directors may require a different presentation style to one targeted at technical purchasers of componentry.

You can describe your own feelings about the creative 'feel' that you are seeking using terms such as 'businesslike', 'imaginative' or 'technical'. There may be creative constraints that you need to impose. For example, it might be essential that the company logo appears prominently or you might be strongly committed to a particular typeface. If the material needs to be produced in several languages, this should be made clear from the beginning, as it can affect the design parameters. It is helpful to indicate what visual material is available for use and in what format. In some media you need to clarify whether you will be producing draft copy or a copy brief and whether or not you expect all the writing to be outsourced.

There are other practical issues to cover. These include any views you have on the type or finish of paper to be used for publications, eg a requirement to use recycled paper or to avoid lamination. You might also have an opinion on content flow and pagination. The proposed production timetable needs to be defined so the supplier can reserve capacity.

The brief should make it absolutely clear what you expect from the supplier. For example, if you are organising an exhibition stand, the brief needs to specify whether you are seeking only a design for the stand or for it to be both designed and built. It should also clarify what you expect to happen next – either a written proposal or a live presentation by a particular date.

Some clients like to state the budget parameters for the project. However, there are some arguments against doing this. Your research should have identified affordable suppliers. If you state a budget, the supplier will tend to work up to that budget when in fact it might have been possible to do the job at a lower cost. If the proposal feels right in other respects but is too expensive, it may be possible to reduce its cost before appointment.

Checklist for supplier briefing

- background to the organisation
- any relevant existing material
- brief description of requirement
- precise definition of supplier role
- purpose of the item
- target audience
- overall feel or style
- creative parameters
- relationship to other items
- corporate identity constraints

- visual material available
- whether it is likely to be translated
- target shelf life for the item
- who will produce copy
- type of paper to use
- any views on finish (eg type and weight of lamination)
- pagination ideas (if any)
- quantity required
- proposed timescale for completion
- what should happen next
- client named contact information

EVENT MANAGEMENT

In addition to managing the events within your own programme, you may be expected to organise activities for other departments. There are some general principles of successful event management that can be applied to a number of the activities you will be organising.

It is important not to commit to dates until venues are identified and reserved. At certain times of the year, the availability of venues is a serious constraint. In London, for example, it can be very difficult to book meeting rooms during the financial reporting season when listed companies are holding preliminary results announcements and annual meetings.

Advance planning is one of the keys to success. Reconnaissance is another. Be sure that you visit the location well in advance and inspect all the facilities and equipment you will be using. Insist that the venue organiser assigns one competent person to coordinate all your requirements. Then put everything in writing and get a confirmation in return.

Attention to detail is crucial and the creation of your own standard event planning sheets will help. Do not be over-ambitious in structuring the event and take particular care to establish a realistic timetable. It is much better to do simple things well and with style than create problems through complexity. This applies to menus, drinks, entertainment, presentations and all aspects of the event.

A few days before the event, go to the venue and put yourself in the mind of a guest arriving and experiencing the occasion. Walk through the process and this will help you to identify any snags and add the touches that will make your guests feel relaxed.

Checklist for event planning

- objectives
- audience
- messages
- budget and plan
- detailed programme
- whether or not partners are invited
- venue
- date and time
- event manager
- invitation format and lists
- directions to venue
- transport and parking
- catering
- audiovisual equipment and operator
- whether or not smoking is permitted
- entertainment or background music
- lighting
- flowers
- guest of honour or speaker
- master of ceremonies
- recall material and gift
- reception, signing-in, name badges if needed
- cloakroom arrangements
- seating and table plans
- direction signs
- photographer
- display material
- media facilities if needed
- rehearsal
- walk-through to check arrangements
- evaluation and report afterwards

SELECTING PROGRAMME ELEMENTS

There are many elements and techniques that can be included in your public relations programmes; this is demonstrated by the sample checklist shown below. In Chapter 4, we analyse some of the issues that affect specific programme elements. The selection and planning of programme content is covered in another book in this series: *Planning and Managing Public Relations Campaigns* by Anne Gregory, 2000.

Checklist of some of the techniques used in public relations programmes

- advertising
- advertorial features
- audiovisual productions
- award programmes
- briefing documents
- briefing meetings
- brochures
- bulletins
- business television
- call centres
- charity support
- community projects
- conferences
- conference calls
- corporate hospitality
- corporate identity
- desktop publishing
- design
- dinners, lunches and receptions
- direct mail
- display stands
- events
- exhibitions
- facility visits
- film
- freelance writers
- information technology
- the Internet
- magazines
- media releases, features, presentations and photocalls
- mementos and gifts
- multimedia presentations

- newsletters
- notice boards
- open days
- overhead and 35mm slides
- photography
- posters
- presentations
- print
- product demonstrations
- project logos and other identifiers
- promotional merchandise
- report and accounts
- research
- seminars
- speeches
- sponsorship
- trademarks
- video
- Web site

4

Managing programme elements

By applying expertise to the detailed activities that make up your programme, you will increase the overall impact and cost-effectiveness of your department's work. Each element in your public relations programme will have different management requirements; some of these are discussed in this chapter.

ADVERTISING AND ADVERTORIALS

Advertising can be a valuable communication tool within an integrated public relations programme. It might be used to reinforce your messages or in situations in which it is the only sure way to deliver your precise message to a target audience. Also, it can provide definitive reference material in journals of record or directories.

Another situation in which you may take out an ad is owing to 'blackmail advertising', when a customer, business partner or the chairperson's favourite charity persuades you to take an insertion.

It is a good idea to have a small selection of timeless, ready-prepared, punchy ads available off the shelf to deal with such situations. This will ensure that the cost of producing a special ad for the occasion is avoided and that you do get some value from the space.

Advertising within marketing communication will usually be handled by the marketing director (though this depends on the nature of your organisation). The world of consumer advertising is very different to the corporate area in terms of budget, style and tone. For this reason, you should select your advertising agency very carefully, using a similar approach to that described for public relations companies in Chapter 12.

You are likely to want crisp and businesslike copy, and you might well know your target audiences and the most cost-effective way of reaching them better than your agency does. This can cause tension between agency copywriters and media teams. Another factor is that corporate public relations budgets tend to fluctuate much more than marketing budgets. Make sure that the agency you select is sensitive to all these issues and consider the smaller shops that are happy to take on this type of work. Well-targeted advertising can fulfil a useful role within your public relations programme if approached in the right way.

You should not scorn paid-for editorial features ('advertorial') as they can deliver valuable exposure if correctly targeted. They are most effective if they are well designed and match the editorial tone and style of the publication in which they appear. They should be well written, preferably by journalists, and illustrated by interesting pictures. Advertorial featuring a message from your chairperson surrounded by laudatory advertisements from your suppliers is best avoided.

AUDIOVISUAL PRODUCTIONS

The use of audiovisual productions in public relations ranges from speaker support slides to the production of expensive corporate films, videos and multimedia presentations.

The first rule about slides is to minimise the number of words and the complexity of illustration. Most speakers put far too much on their slides. Your slides will have extra value if all your presentations are produced to the same standard and can be combined together in the future. Therefore you should include a standard design in your communication manual and make sure that your production house uses it. This will also avoid cost arising from the creation of a new basic design approach for every presentation.

The costs of film, video, multimedia and other audiovisual formats vary enormously. Select your supplier carefully using the approach described earlier. Ensure that your brief is clear and that it lists any points or visuals that must be included within the creative route adopted. In the brief and the production contract you must specify the widest relevant parameters of how and where you might use the material, otherwise you may find that there are contractual constraints.

You may be able to reduce the cost of video production dramatically by using an independent producer rather than an integrated production house. They will work with you in selecting a director, the talent (including presenter), the technical production team and the studios. Using this route, you can often put together a team that suits your needs better, as production companies may be locked into long-term relationships.

A key stage in video production is agreement regarding the 'treatment' that outlines the content of the programme. Scripting can be an emotional issue if you find yourself working with a temperamental writer or director. Here – as in all other creative support – you must remember that you are paying for the programme and it has to be accurate and meet your requirements. This is far more important than winning creative awards.

BRIEFING DOCUMENTS

Throughout your programmes you will be making use of briefing documents. These will range from papers for Ministers and Members of Parliament to internal briefs for your own management. It is important to keep such documents free from jargon and make them as short as possible. If you cannot keep the size down to two pages, provide an executive summary with the main arguments presented in 'bullet point' style.

Where appropriate, make sure that your presentation team is equipped with a question-and-answer document. This should cover all the questions your target audience might ask, including the most difficult specialist questions that might not be covered in your core document, which is intended for a wider audience. Such question-and-answer briefs are usually restricted to internal circulation for those people authorised to issue information, and they should be boldly labelled to clarify this.

Develop short positioning statements on all planned or possible future major announcements and potentially difficult issues for use if stories break unexpectedly. It is also useful to hold on file descriptions of your organisation in a range of lengths. These should begin with a one-sentence positioning statement and might include versions of 100 words, 200 words and a full-length media feature of around 1,000 words. You may be surprised at how frequently this standing copy will provide a base for modification and enable you to respond rapidly to a variety of requests.

BROCHURES

Your organisation may need a corporate brochure or other *ad hoc* publications. Before you begin the production process you will need a brief describing the publication's purpose, audience, creative parameters, anticipated shelf life, corporate identity constraints, budget and other factors that will enable the chosen supplier to meet your needs.

If you rarely produce brochures, you will need to select a supplier from a broad field. If you have a regular requirement, it will be worth identifying a small number of preferred suppliers of different sizes and creative capabilities from which you invite perhaps two or three to pitch for each job.

Some organisations commission creative design and production from a design agency and then buy the print themselves. The danger in this approach is that if there is a problem, the printer will blame the designer's print brief and the designer will blame the printer's capability or quality procedures. It is better to pay a print-management fee to the design house to control the whole project for you. In this way, you can still have a strong say in the print quotes, but the designer will ensure that the printer has the necessary capability. The print-management fee is likely to be lower if you agree with the designer that you will settle the printer's invoice direct after the designer has verified it.

CORPORATE IDENTITY

However large or small your organisation is, it will need a document or manual that defines the typography and graphic representation of its name, logo and other visual identification. This has to be reinforced by a manual that describes how the identity is applied to everything your organisation utilises – from stationery and product packaging to premises and vehicles.

This subject could occupy a chapter or a book to itself. To summarise, the main tasks are to ensure that you have a set of practical rules that are endorsed by senior management and communicated throughout your organisation, and that everyone knows where to go for guidance on compliance. You need to allocate responsibility to a member of your team for regularly monitoring general compliance with corporate identity rules.

However powerful your basic identity might be, the detailed execution and application rules need to be reviewed occasionally – perhaps every 10 years or so. This can be a highly emotional experience internally and may attract a great deal of external attention if decisions and costs are difficult to justify. Avoid change for its own sake, but ensure that your corporate identity remains a valid representation of your organisation, which should be a living and developing organism in a changing environment.

Some suppliers in this field have wildly ambitious ideas about the budgets required to carry out the design work for the basic elements and applications manual. However, there are excellent design companies around that will do a professional job for a realistic price. If you do not need the glamour of association with a famous corporate identity designer, you may be surprised by the bargains that are available.

When a large organisation decides to change or update its corporate identity, the decision generates a further major project: to manage the implementation. The project team will need to include representatives of many functions. Changes to buildings and vehicle identification are expensive and need to be planned well in advance, utilising existing maintenance budgets wherever possible. In some industries, it is necessary to modify the manufacturing tooling that places a logo on the product.

Your organisation may utilise a number of trademarks and these must be registered and protected. Usually, this is the responsibility of the company secretary or legal department, but you should make sure that you understand the situation and become involved if necessary.

EXHIBITIONS AND DISPLAYS

The first task is to define your objectives for attending an exhibition. Attendance at major exhibitions can be extremely expensive. Be sure that you need to spend the money and that you are unable to get the impact you need by holding a parallel event at another venue or by attending and circulating without a stand.

Some reasons for exhibiting

- launching a new product or service
- establishing a position in a new market
- demonstrating commitment to industry or market
- improving customer contact and generating sales leads
- building awareness and gaining media coverage

Once you have decided to attend, you will need a well-structured brief for your exhibition stand designer, as with other creative projects.

The sky can be the limit in terms of design and build costs, so set a realistic budget and insist that it is achieved. Your costs will be particularly high if you are building a stand on the open floor rather than taking space in a shell scheme constructed by the exhibition organisers. If you are planning to attend a series of exhibitions, it may pay you to create a standard display that can be stored and transported to each venue.

Ensure that the stand staff keep a record of all visitors so that you can assess the value of participation and add the contacts to your database. Any new business enquiries or other visitor requests should be logged on a form for this purpose so that follow-up can be initiated and monitored.

Consider producing a simple standard corporate display utilising a lightweight modular system that can easily be transported in a car. This can be used at a range of events, from careers days to seminars, and might even brighten up your reception area between events.

MAGAZINES, NEWSLETTERS AND BULLETINS

In-house magazines, newsletters and bulletins can be useful elements in your communication programmes. You should ensure that the purpose of such publications and their editorial policy is clearly defined. You may have to compromise eventually and attempt to reach different audiences with the same publication, but the danger is that the resultant product appeals to none.

The value of these publications to your internal communication process depends on the structure of your organisation, the access that your employees have to your news on the Internet and the efficiency of your internal cascade briefing system.

There has to be a realistic assessment of the depth of interest your readers will have. For example, many employees will have a general interest in their work and their employer's plans, but will obviously want to know what effect change is likely to have on their own rewards, working conditions and job security.

It can be difficult to set the right tone in an internal publication for a multi-site organisation. You may want to make it more interesting by including human interest stories, but if the employees in Germany do not know the employees in Wales, are they really going to be interested in their marriages and babies? This problem is compounded if you assume that everyone reads English, or that they can be bothered to do so if the interest is marginal. On the other hand, there is a natural desire for employees to read about themselves and people they know or can relate to. This might be best handled through local newsletters or slip editions. Focus groups, survey forms, telephone interviews or structured research can be used to test reader attitudes.

It is unlikely that a publication appealing to your employees will also interest a wide external audience. In fact, there is a proliferation of junk print and those who really do want to follow your activities can do so by accessing your Web site. Because of this, you may find it necessary to target the external circulation of your publications to a small, controlled list of stakeholders who have a real and direct relationship with your organisation. You can still mail it to others who make a specific request. Send a reply-paid re-registration card to such opt-in readers from time to time to check whether they are still at the same address and interested.

When producing a publication, you will need to decide which part of the production process to handle in-house and which to buy out-of-house. There are suppliers who will do everything for you and there is the option of doing everything except print in-house. Usually, the most cost-effective route is to produce editorial in-house using your own team and freelance writers where necessary, while outsourcing design and production.

Avoid the all too common mistake of producing a superbly designed periodical that is three months out of date by the time it is issued. Before embarking on an expensive publishing project, consider whether the need could be filled by a simple bulletin produced internally with the advantage of speed and low cost.

MEMENTOS AND GIFTS

Although the concept of providing business gifts is now generally out of favour, there are occasions when a small memento of an occasion is appropriate. This might apply to the completion of a major project by a company, a facility opening or an important anniversary.

There are numerous suppliers of mementos who advertise in the industry media. You need to ensure that the intrinsic value of such items is not significant and that its value falls below any ethical limits set for the recipients by their own organisations. This is a subjective area, but mementos should be both low cost *and* classy. Any company identification should be applied tastefully. Always consider how you and your chief executive would react if given the item by someone else. Would it be immediately junked?

Many organisations keep a small supply of low-cost utilitarian items such as pens and golf umbrellas to give to visitors or to distribute at routine events. These can normally carry a prominent logo or company name without causing offence.

PHOTOGRAPHY

You will have specific photographic requirements to support various elements in your programmes. This issue needs to be given constant attention, otherwise you will find that when you are producing a report and accounts, brochure or audiovisual, you will need shots of recent activities that cannot be recaptured.

Photographing people, events and facilities requires different skills. Brochure photography is different from news photography. You should identify several photographers with different aptitudes who can be called on when needed. It is worthwhile having a departmental camera to take your own shots of smaller events and for when your team is travelling around the organisation.

Whether you should specify transparency, print or digital media for origination of your pictures will depend on the technical and creative issues relating to their intended use. The ability to manipulate images cheaply and transmit them by e-mail are huge benefits of new technology. Much of your material should be held electronically for these reasons, however it was initiated. You will need to install appropriate software to give a satisfactory standard for e-mail transmission. Take advice from the suppliers and recipients with whom you are likely to be working in this way.

It will be very useful if you can find a local supplier of commercial photographic processing services who can produce your prints, move shots between media and manipulate images.

PRESENTATIONS, CONFERENCES AND SEMINARS

Presentations by your management team to small groups is one of the most valuable communication tools. Be well prepared and well rehearsed and agree in advance the question-and-answer brief and who will answer which questions.

Utilise visual aids such as slides, flipcharts or acetates, but avoid long videos or audiovisual presentations when presenting to small senior groups. If the audience knows very little about your organisation, it is acceptable to show a short, factual audiovisual to position the organisation correctly. Keep the formal proceedings as short as possible commensurate with stating your case.

When you are relying on technical hardware such as a data projector, it does no harm to have an overhead projector in reserve for any emergency together with back-up copies of your spare visuals on acetate. Always keep spare bulbs, fuses and copies of the operating instructions with all your equipment.

Do everything possible to put yourself in the minds of your audience when planning your meetings. For example, if you are presenting to a small group of fund managers, speak to your contact to discover how much time has been allocated for the meeting in their diaries and the format that will suit them best. If you are using your audience's premises or an outside venue, gain as much information as you can about the room and clarify in writing who is providing what equipment, the power points that are available and other logistical needs.

Think carefully before mixing audiences. It might be unhelpful for your suppliers to hear your clients complaining about your high profit margins, for example.

You should consider whether the best way of getting your message across would be to organise or sponsor conferences or seminars. These would involve external speakers who could provide your target audience with complementary information to your own. This can be a way of attracting a wider attendance and building your reputation as an industry leader.

Aim to provide a short, punchy recall document for your audience. If you are using slides, either give copies to the audience at the beginning so that they can make notes on them or announce that they will be available at the end. It is most annoying to attendees if they are not familiar with the form and have to make extensive notes just in case. Do not distribute a huge pack of brochures unless they really are needed for future reference. Too much material is distributed only to be binned as soon as people get back to their offices. Do have a selection of brochures available at the back for people who really want them.

If you need to reach a small but widespread audience at short notice to deal with a breaking story, a video- or telephone-conference call can be a highly effective method. It will minimise the inconvenience for your audience and the time required from your own management, leaving them free to deal with the substance of the issue.

Whether to use verbatim speeches or to speak from bullet points at all these events will depend upon the formality of the occasion and the information to be communicated. The natural style of your management and their ability to stay on message have to be considered. It is almost always safest to speak from a verbatim text, but even when this is done it is easiest to first agree the content structure in bullet-point form. A useful tip is to write the speech in a large font, ready for reading, setting it at a size and spacing that means each page is approximately equal to one minute of delivery. This helps you to keep to the target length as you write your way through the outline structure. Few aspects of a speech can please an audience more than brevity. This is even more vital when you are a speaker at an external event.

REPORT AND ACCOUNTS

If you work for a public company, the production of the report and accounts will be one of the most demanding and hazardous tasks. It has to be mailed on a particular day and there will be many people involved during the production process. These will include your management, the finance department, the audit firm, the company secretary's team and the operating management, who will all have an interest.

If you are responsible, do not underestimate the importance and size of this task. It might occupy one member of your team almost full-time for three or four months. It is the company's most public document and may generate considerable emotion. It has to be right legally, it has to be on time and it has to satisfy your management as well as the shareholders and financial analysts.

It is vital to start early and to establish schedules covering all stages that are communicated to, and accepted by, all those involved. The process, from agreeing the strategic positioning of the report through design concept to mailing, can be tortuous and will involve many author's corrections. These need to be minimised because they are expensive and can jeopardise the mailing date.

This is often seen by suppliers as an area for rich margins, so it is well worth shopping around initially and then putting the job out to pitch regularly. However, you should be very cautious about using a supplier with no experience in this field. The earlier reference to the importance of using your design house to project manage your brochure print is particularly relevant to such an important publication.

Even if you are not a public company, there can be benefits to producing an annual report of your activities that you can mail to customers, suppliers and other interested parties. You can include useful background material on your sector, which will give the publication added credibility.

RESEARCH

You should be using market and opinion research as part of your continuing evaluation process and you will have additional specific requirements from time to time. There are long-term tracking studies of the attitudes of various audiences that will enable you to monitor your position in a consistent way. The cost is relatively low because these are produced for a number of companies on a collaborative basis. You are more likely to get a better response from your target audience from an established study conducted for a number of clients at the same time.

Where your needs are more specific, you will need to put together a brief explaining what you are trying to achieve and ask several research companies to respond with a proposal. Designing questionnaires and sampling procedures is a highly specialist field so do take the advice of the professionals.

The use of 'dipstick' research techniques or self-completion questionnaires may only be marginally better than doing no research at all. The results of such informal procedures should be treated with caution.

The public relations industry has attempted to introduce a standardised approach to the evaluation of campaign effectiveness – details are available from the IPR. There is little point in spending money on public relations if you have no means of assessing its effects and reporting to your management.

Sometimes, a research project is commissioned with the main purpose of obtaining indirect publicity for an organisation through publication of the results in the media or by direct mail. This can be a useful programme element or it can result in a cynical response if the project is not well structured and conducted by a recognised research company.

SPONSORSHIP AND AWARDS

Sponsorship activity can range from adding your name to an event that will attract worldwide media coverage to putting it on the shirts of a local youth tennis team.

Be sure you know what you are buying in terms of target audience exposure and costs compared to other ways of spending your money. Buy the main action of a smaller event rather than become one of 20 secondary sponsors of a major event, none of whom may get any worthwhile coverage.

Organising or sponsoring award programmes can be beneficial. It is only worthwhile to sponsor your own award programme if it really can establish credibility in your sector. This may be more realistic if you link with a leading publication, professional body or trade association. Sponsoring one of a whole list of awards at someone else's event is only worth doing if you can extract value at a sensible cost. It might actually exclude you from entering your own organisation and winning an award.

Consider how the activity you are sponsoring can be used for a corporate hospitality programme for other target audiences. Use your imagination to get extra value. If you are sponsoring a racing car, consider putting it on display for your employees and explaining to them why you are involved. Keep them informed of progress.

Remember that even altruistic donations to charity can be made in a way that brings recognition to your organisation. Put a plaque on the equipment you have financed, for example, and hand it over with a photo shoot. Try to resist pouring your budget into your manager's favourite interest, even though this might be difficult.

WEB SITE

Your Web site is one of the most important and cost-effective elements in your communication programmes. You need to organise it in such a way that it attracts your target audiences. Care is needed to avoid an unmanageable flood of worldwide enquiries from irrelevant groups. Of course, it doesn't matter if these groups simply look at your pages, as long as no response requirement is triggered. The information on your site must be consistent with your other media and must be kept right up to date. Drawing material from standard sources such as your news releases, annual report or company magazine reduces this task.

Your organisation may be using its Web site for many purposes, from electronic trading to supplier scheduling through a limited-access area. You might also use limited-access areas for communication with employees, retailers, distributors and other audiences.

You may be involved in these areas, but the public pages are your particular concern.

As in other creative areas, you will find enormous variation in the cost and quality of suppliers – personal recommendation from a trusted source is a good start. Costs can be surprisingly low if you select carefully. There are advantages to using one supplier to register domain names, organise hosting and access, design your site content and maintain it to an up-to-date condition.

You should take care to register all domain names that you might wish to use in the future as others may 'steal' them from you and offer them for sale at a ransom price. The way in which your site is hosted and accessed will influence costs and administration, and your supplier should offer you a range of options. Decisions on content need to take account of the universal access to the public area. Any useful information will be accessed immediately by competitors and a comprehensive list of the management team is a gift to headhunters. You will need to put in place administrative systems for analysing visits to the site and managing enquiries that need a response.

The role of information technology in the administration of your department is reviewed in Chapter 13. You should also be able to use the Internet as a valuable research resource to keep up to date with industry trends, government announcements, competitors, suppliers, new markets and all the issues that impinge on your activities.

5

The departmental plan

ESTABLISHING THE LONG-TERM STRATEGY

The fundamental task of public relations strategic planning and programme planning is the subject of another book in this series (*Planning and Managing Public Relations Campaigns* by Anne Gregory). If public relations is to be of any value to an organisation, it must take its rightful place within the overall strategic development plan. There will always be emergencies and new situations to test the public relations manager. It is essential, however, that you avoid getting bogged down in short-term issues and do keep a clear vision of a long-term purpose.

That long-term vision should address the basic task of reputation management as defined earlier. This must be related to the specific situation and needs of your own organisation, and must begin with your involvement in and clear understanding of the organisation's long-term strategic business plan. Your own long-term plan must also take account of the current reputation of the organisation, analysed through structured research and anecdotal evidence. The reputation of the organisation may be better or worse than reality and reality may be better or worse than the management believes. The use of external structured research will help to minimise emotional reactions to the appraisal.

In addition to managing the organisation's overall reputation there will be specific initiatives in the organisation's strategic plan which require public relations support. For example, a business may plan to enter a new market, perhaps Japan, in three years' time. The public relations plan will have to include an appraisal of the current awareness, if any, of the company in Japan, the special nature of the public relations environment in Japan and the steps needed to build the appropriate level of awareness to support market entry and sustain a presence subsequently.

In developing the long-term public relations plan and presenting it to management, it is important to bear in mind that a good reputation can be destroyed in minutes but can take years to create or restore. It is important not to promise too much too soon. The speed of achievement will be partly influenced by the resource deployed, but there is a point at which excessive expenditure may make little difference or even become counterproductive.

As well as establishing a long-term strategic public relations plan, it is vital that the department maintains a crisis communications plan. At minimum this should define the procedures to be followed by the public relations team if the organisation experiences a sudden emergency. This plan should be communicated throughout the organisation. A well-managed organisation will have a detailed plan for crisis management incorporating the public relations dimension. If this is not the case, the public relations team should work to persuade general management to face up to this task.

Typical contents list for corporate departmental plan

- Executive summary.
- Review of progress against previous plan.
- Budget performance.
- Budget proposals.
- Critical issues and strategy.
- Financial communication.
- Government affairs.

- Marketing communication.
- Internal communication.
- Community relations.
- Specific technique strategies, such as creative strategy, media relations, audiovisual, etc.
- Departmental structure and development.

In each area of public relations you should include analysis, issues, objectives, strategies and action plans.

THE ANNUAL DEPARTMENTAL PLAN

Each year you will need to put together a plan for the following year and get it agreed with your general manager. It should also be presented formally to the entire senior management team for your organisation so that they also feel they own the plan. It should indicate how the elements of the long-term plan will be progressed during the year ahead and what strategies and actions will be included.

The departmental plan will need to support developments in the operations during the year based on discussions with your general manager, other departments and subsidiary activities. If your role is within a subsidiary or a regional office it will have to reflect the needs and views of the principal operation.

The departmental budget should be presented at the same time, indicating the resources required to carry out the plan. This will help to establish the link between actions, results and cost. Most organisations have a budget planning period when you will be asked to submit your proposals. You may be asked to achieve specified cost-reduction targets. In any case, it is important to link the work you do to its purpose and cost so that your general manager understands the consequence of reducing the budget or denying a requested increase.

PERSONAL ACTION PLANS

The departmental team is more likely to be well motivated if each member has an agreed personal action plan for the year ahead.

Apart from providing a clear purpose to the year's work, the plan will establish a good basis for reviewing individual performance in the annual appraisal.

The personal plans should together cover all the actions that are necessary to complete the departmental plan for the year. They should be discussed and agreed with each individual who can then accept accountability for their part in the programme.

Obviously there will be a substantial element of continuing activity for most team members and it should not be necessary to document this. There are certain to be unexpected events to which the team will need to react, so capacity needs to be retained for these. The personal plans should concentrate on change, and should indicate activities which are to be changed or reviewed during the year and new tasks which have been identified.

The most effective way of presenting the personal plans is in the form of a simple spreadsheet (see Table 5.1). This should be in columns defining each action in simple terms, who is responsible, a target date for completion and a space for the status update and other comments. This simple format will facilitate regular review which might be carried out with the team members monthly or quarterly.

MONITORING AND REPORTING PERFORMANCE

The systems used for monitoring and reporting performance upwards will depend on the size of the department, the nature of the tasks and the customs of the organisation. You may be required to submit a monthly or quarterly report to your general manager in a particular format. Whatever systems your manager follows, you will always be able to give a good account of your activities if you maintain sound reporting systems within your own department.

Your subordinates should provide you with a brief activity report each month. Such reports are best presented in bullet point format with a consistent structure. It is valuable to report on the quantity of work done as well as the outcome because

Table 5.1 *Sample extracts from action plan monitor*

Action	Resp	Month	Status
Financial communication			
Arrange media training for chairperson	SW	3	Completed
Complete proposals for analysts' visit to Paris factory	CW	5	Seeking views of analysts
Presentation to potential US investors	SW	7	Researching current attitudes. New York location identified
Research lender attitudes to the company	CW	11	Draft research brief due month 7
Internal communication			
Launch new-look employee magazine	GG	3	Now scheduled for month 5 to cover annual results
Identify venue for annual management conference	MDM	2	Completed
Theme recommendations for management conference to CEO	MDM	5	First draft being reviewed within department
Review communication on suggestion scheme	GG	8	Awaiting resource
Joint review of strategies with personnel department	MDM	10	Date proposed to personnel team
Corporate programmes			
Re-design Internet pages	KOS	2	Completed
Agree brief for new corporate brochure	KOS	5	Department brainstorm planned for month 5
Design matrix of standard media features	SW	7	Awaiting resource
Complete plan for centenary celebration	RB	11	Working group membership agreed. Meeting arranged with CEO to agree budget parameters

the logistics of public relations work is little understood by line management and because you may wish to include a summary in your own report at some time. For example, you may record the number of media calls dealt with or the number of brochure copies requested.

The question of evaluation of public relations work is covered in another book in this series (*Planning and Managing Public Relations Campaigns*, Anne Gregory, 2000). Briefly, the evaluation process should first measure whether the programme was implemented successfully – for example, whether media exposure was obtained or who attended the seminar. The next stage is to use opinion research to test whether the target audience became better informed than before and whether attitudes to the organisation improved. The ultimate purpose of public relations is to affect behaviour, so the final stage of evaluation is to examine whether this happened. Did the investors buy the shares or was the recruitment programme successful? Practitioners should beware of evaluation processes which attempt to draw conclusions from media coverage or some other aspect of programme evaluation in isolation.

Measurement criteria
- whether programme completed satisfactorily
- effect on awareness
- effect on attitude
- behavioural change

COMMUNICATING YOUR STRATEGIES TO YOUR COLLEAGUES

In order to maximise support for your department you should take every opportunity to ensure that your colleagues around the organisation understand its purpose and current activities.

Take every opportunity to present your activities formally to management groups around the organisation, especially to subsidiary boards if you are working for a business. Make sure that public relations is included on the agenda for any management conferences which are held. Take care to present your wares professionally as in your function you will be expected to perform well, but avoid extravagant expenditure on the presentation which might attract criticism.

The more your value to the organisation is recognised, the easier it will be to win support for your plans and budgets. The allies you gain will be an additional and valuable resource for carrying your messages to your target audiences.

6

Managing your budgets

GENERAL APPROACH

Establishing and controlling your budget must take account of the general management approach to public relations expenditure. First, it is possible that your manager will have a low awareness of the public relations function. He or she may also suspect that the activity is a luxury, an expensive overhead.

It is vital, therefore, to link your budget submission to your departmental plan. You need to demonstrate the link between the objectives, action programme and targeted results. It is equally important that you demonstrate outstanding management control once the budget is agreed. You must understand the detail of your expenditure, be able to answer any possible questions from your management and never give them surprises. It is also important to work closely with the financial controller who produces your management accounts and win their respect for your professionalism.

WHAT TO INCLUDE

It is almost certain that your organisation will have a standard form for budget submissions and that it will be issued to you with guidelines on what to include. Some items such as office space rental or stationery might be budgeted centrally or by department. In any event, unless you are setting up a new department, your starting point may be the previous year's budget submission and actual expenditure so far in the year. Normally, the finance department will issue guidelines covering such matters as standard inflation factors you may include or cost-reduction targets you have to meet. If you hope to get more money than these guidelines imply, you will have to put up good arguments.

When budgeting for the cost of your people, you will need to include such items as salaries, any bonus applicable, cars, pensions and other benefits, state insurance and out-of-pocket expenses. The finance department will normally give you detailed help with this. Do not forget to budget for your own salary unless it is the company's policy for it to be absorbed at the next level up in the structure.

You will need to ensure that items such as computer services, heating and lighting, photocopying, postage, telephones and all the other administration costs and internal charges are included in your budget or covered centrally.

The cost of all the services and goods you purchase externally will be a major part of your budget. There are options for the way in which you list these in your budget. You might show them by area of public relations activity such as financial communication, government affairs, and so on.

One problem with this approach is that it is unlikely to provide enough detail and costs will be difficult to allocate. For example, a corporate brochure will be used across all your programmes. Media relations activity is likely to be aimed at a variety of audiences. Another approach is to categorise the budget by type of expenditure such as advertising or brochures.

There is no single answer to this and much depends on precedent and organisation policy. The list below shows the budget headings which one corporate public relations department has found convenient for its own cost-centre analysis. No two corporate departments have precisely the same spread of responsibility, so no two budget structures are the same. The example combines the alternative approaches described, allocating costs to specific target audiences where this is easily done. Each major area is divided into subheadings.

Example of corporate department budget structure

Salaries and other employee costs:

- salaries
- bonuses
- national insurance
- company pension contributions
- health insurance and other benefits
- company cars
- temporary staff
- training and professional development

Travel and personal expenses:

- air travel
- other travel
- subsistence
- entertaining
- professional subscriptions including IPR
- telephones
- other

Office supplies, services and computing:

- allocated overheads including rental
- equipment leases
- depreciation of capital equipment
- stationery and other office supplies
- computer supplies and services
- telephone and fax
- postage
- monitoring services
- distribution services

Financial communication programmes:

- report and accounts and interim statements

- annual general meeting
- shareholder and broker meetings and visits
- financial results advertising
- financial communication consultancy

Government affairs programmes:

- contact events and visits
- monitoring services
- government relations consultancy

Marketing communication programmes:

- product literature
- product audiovisual
- product advertising
- exhibitions
- sales promotion
- product launches
- marketing communication consultancy

Internal communication programmes:

- employee publications
- e-mail and fax distribution services
- management and employee briefing conferences
- employee award schemes
- internal communication consultancy

Community relations programmes:

- open days and other community events
- local sponsorship
- subscriptions and donations

Corporate activities:

- corporate identity
- communication manuals
- group advertising
- brochures and other literature

- display material
- promotional merchandise
- audiovisual
- Web site
- photography
- media relations
- periodical publications
- corporate events and hospitality
- sponsorship
- opinion research
- general public relations consultancy services

In practice, it is necessary to agree the number of separate cost-centre reporting headings with the management accountant in the finance department because of the potential administrative costs of the detailed analysis. In any event, the department's own records can be maintained in this detailed way.

CAPITAL EXPENDITURE

In addition, you will need to budget for items of capital expenditure such as furniture, computers and audiovisual equipment. You may need to cover any company cars you control under this heading. Make sure that you are included in whatever system your employer operates for budgeting capital expenditure. Sometimes public relations is forgotten because the requirements are usually relatively small. If your needs have been left out of the total capital budget it can be a battle to obtain them, but when budgeted it should be a matter of routine.

CONTROL AND MONITORING

Everything you purchase under your budget will need to be ordered formally in writing, often utilising a standard purchase order form. The invoices you receive will need to be properly checked and authorised, coded according to your financial systems and passed to the accounts department to be processed and paid. Keep copies of all your approved invoices and internal charges, filed by cost centre.

Check your monthly management accounts carefully to reconcile these approved invoices against your reported expenditure. If you cannot reconcile the report with your expectations, query this immediately with the accounts department. If you cannot agree, continue to pursue the matter until you do because you are accountable for your own budget. You will get nowhere by questioning the accounts at the end of the year. This principle applies equally to any internal charges you dispute. Do not allow anyone to make charges against your budget without your agreement and authority. Where issues cannot be resolved with the finance department you must take them to your manager for resolution.

You will need to establish clearly and in writing which members of your team have authority to commit your department to expenditure and to approve invoices and other charges. This must be documented to the finance department so that no invoices are paid without the correct authority. Wherever possible, avoid allowing more than one person to approve invoices against any specific cost centre. Follow this policy and the accountability for budget compliance will be clear and there will be no misunderstandings.

CALENDARISED BUDGETS

You will be required, or should choose, to produce a schedule forecasting how much of your budget will be spent in each calendar month. Some items such as salaries may be spread evenly across the year and others, such as a new brochure, will occur in specific months. Each month review how you are performing against this calendarised budget and be ready to explain any variances, either up or down, and how they will come back into line. If you are showing an adverse variance, your manager will ask you to explain how it will be recovered. If you are showing a positive variance, you may be challenged to surrender this saving, so be prepared.

FORECASTING YOUR BUDGET PERFORMANCE

At all times you need to understand: your expenditure to date as reported in the management accounts; the value of invoices you have approved which are in the system but not yet appearing in your accounts; the cost of all commitments you have made which have not yet been invoiced; and the balance of your budget which is still available to support your plans. Use of a schedule utilising the headings shown in Table 6.1 will help you in your budget control.

Table 6.1   *Budget monitoring and control chart*

| Cost centre | Period 6 budget analysis (£000s) | | | | |
	Reported spend to date	Future spend committed	Total spent and committed	Total budget for year	Balance available to spend
Salaries and other employee costs	146	147	293	302	9
Travel and personal expenses	9	3	12	27	15
Office supplies, services and computing	29	22	51	53	2
Financial communication programmes	32	63	95	112	17
Government affairs programmes	7	11	18	29	11
Marketing communication programmes	94	65	159	169	10
Internal communication programmes	48	49	97	115	18
Community relations programmes	14	16	30	30	–
Corporate activities	51	61	112	124	12
Total	430	437	867	961	94

It is particularly important to have a tight grip and to use a forecasting schedule of this type as the financial year end approaches. Be sure that you instruct all your suppliers to bill you promptly at the year end. Advise your finance department of any outstanding invoices so that they can include these in the year-end provisions. If you fail to do this you will lose some of your budget for the following year to pay for the previous year's costs.

Ensure that you spend your budget wisely by regularly obtaining competing quotes for everything you buy. Although you will be using specialist services which cannot always be purchased like stationery or heating oil, you should still find ways to test the market to ensure that you are buying them cost effectively.

Finally, remember the question of value added or sales taxes on your purchases. Normally you will do all your budgeting net of such taxes but make sure that you understand your organisation's policy on this and that you look at all transactions on the appropriate basis.

DEALING WITH UNBUDGETED EXPENDITURE

You must avoid giving unpleasant surprises to your management. If you propose to incur unbudgeted expenditure for a new initiative, you must present the plan formally to your manager, indicating the additional costs. Obtain formal approval for the additional budget and ensure that you record this in a note to your manager and to the finance department.

Examples of legitimate reasons for unbudgeted expenditure
- merger and acquisition activity
- defence against takeover bid
- issue of new shares
- raising new loans
- impact of unexpected legislation
- taxation increases
- crisis communication management
- product recall communication
- support programme for newly appointed chief executive
- communication programme when company wins award

If the cost of an approved plan looks as if it will exceed the budget, you should let your management know this immediately and then write confirming the fact, indicating any proposals you can develop to recover the situation through savings elsewhere.

Sometimes your management will request you to carry out an additional activity which will adversely affect your budget. You may be asked to support an unexpected business initiative or perhaps to provide sponsorship for a director's particular area of interest. The appropriate action is to write a note to your manager indicating the amount of the additional expenditure and stating that it is outside your approved budget and that you assume that this will be treated as an approved budget over-run. Once the position is clear, make sure that the finance department is informed.

Meticulous financial control will probably do more to enhance your reputation as a manager than any other performance measurement.

Ten top tips for budget confidence

- demonstrate outstanding financial control
- take great care with your budget submission
- don't forget capital items
- have a clear and single authority for each cost centre
- keep a copy of all invoices you approve
- do not accept charges you have not approved
- maintain a constant forecast of expenditure
- regularly obtain competitive quotes from suppliers
- get written approval for budget variations
- never give your manager an unpleasant budget surprise

7

Delivering value for money

ORGANISING FOR VALUE

The previous chapter reviewed the procedures which you should establish in order to create and control your budget, however large or small it may be. This is an important start but good financial management goes beyond these procedures and your department can be organised in such a way that it will be able to deliver exceptional value for money.

Unless your general manager is very unusual, good departmental organisation will ensure that the value you produce for the company is reflected in the way in which you are valued by your employers. Apart from bringing a great deal of job satisfaction, being highly valued by the company's management will help to further your career.

MOTIVATING YOUR TEAM TO SAVE MONEY

Whether you have 1 person in your department or 20, make sure that they all know that value for money is an important measure of their performance. Give as much praise to your team for a good cost-saving idea as you do for an exceptionally well-written news release or a great cover for a brochure. You should also ensure that they know that their achievements in this area are discussed with the senior management and mention cost control in annual appraisals.

Paying attention to small items of expenditure is important, but this is not the same as being miserly about the minutiae. Excessive penny-pinching can be counterproductive, in fact, because it demotivates the team and brings the process into disrepute. Worrying about an extra jar of coffee from the petty cash when the team has worked late would be stupid. Getting a mailshot on one page instead of two, however, can make a real saving in print and postage costs.

Columns of figures in the management accounts can seem unreal when it is someone else's money and therefore you should encourage your team to treat their employer's money as carefully as they would their own. Find ways of reminding the team that this is real cash which has to be earned by your organisation. In some cases it may help your team's understanding if you relate your costs to real-life examples. Point out, for example, that producing a brochure can be as expensive as buying two family cars.

TAKE A FREE RIDE WHEN YOU CAN

In many organisations central services covering areas such as document printing, computer support, stationery and postage, are available to you. If these services are not recharged to your budget or are covered by a fixed charge, make the maximum use of them provided they meet your requirements. If they meet your needs after modification, work to persuade the manager responsible to make the necessary adjustments.

On the other hand, you may be charged for central services which you are compelled to use and which are inefficient or uncompetitively priced. In such cases try to get the charges reduced or win the freedom to buy outside. Do remember that such an approach will ensure that other departments take a similar look at any charges you impose on them.

Take every opportunity within the rules of the organisation to charge your costs on to other people, having first obtained their budget approval. This might include costs you have incurred on behalf of subsidiary companies in supporting their programmes. If you pay for the employee magazine and also send it to pensioners, you might persuade the pension fund administrator to meet the mailing cost.

GETTING VALUE FROM YOUR PEOPLE

Achieving the right blend in your team will enable you to get the best value from them. By balancing ages, experience, professionally qualified practitioners and support staff, you can establish the most cost-effective balance. Including young, newly qualified practitioners will give your operation a dynamism at low cost. In a small operation you will have to accept that they may move on to get more responsibility, but then you can pull them back later when you need someone with more experience. This way you will also save on recruitment costs.

It is useful to have several part-time employees or self-employed consultants who can work extra hours when necessary. This is much better value than staffing your department to meet peak workloads. Of course, you should also use your public relations consultancy in this way. Setting up the right balance between a retainer and project fees will have a significant effect on costs.

Planning the training for your team on a long-term basis will save money. Identify some standard courses, such as the IPR workshops, to satisfy core requirements for professional development. Wherever possible, set up shared training sessions attended by several team members – for example, on advanced usage of your standard office software. Make all the use you can of any courses covering general office and management skills that have been organised by your personnel department.

Personal expenses

Few people in public relations behave in a way to justify the function's image in some quarters for lavish personal expenses. Nevertheless, it is worth looking for ways to stretch the budget.

Air travel costs can be an emotional subject and absorb much of the expenses budget in global companies. Establishing working relationships based on personal contact is important for communicators. This should be balanced with the use of telephone conference calls, video conferencing and e-mail for rapid contact. Better travel deals can often be found in the package holiday brochures than in the business travel department. Your favourite airline might be offering a holiday package including hotel accommodation in the city you plan to visit. Often the travel times will be unsuitable on such deals but whoever books your office travel should know that you expect such options to be investigated.

In recent years there has been a trend in Europe to replicate the excellent low-cost hotels which are available in so many parts of the United States. Costing less than half the price of more traditional properties, these simple but clean and modern facilities with an adjoining restaurant are often close to motorways.

Keeping contact with the team is essential but mobile phones are expensive and it is easy to use them excessively. Usage should be monitored regularly. A limited number of key team members will have an allocated mobile phone, but the other needs in the office can usually be met by having one spare mobile which is shared.

OFFICE COSTS

The general administration costs of the office can consume 5 or 10 per cent of your budget, so give the responsibility for managing this budget to one determined member of your team.

Stationery and related items should be purchased competitively and used in a well-managed way. Competitive and attractive deals are now available on telephone service in the UK and other countries.

Making effective use of information technology (IT) is one of the best ways to save money around the office. However, IT can also be a financial drain unless you make sure that it is actively managed by a well-trained member of your staff. It is particularly important to minimise the use of expensive consultants to develop special software such as customised databases. Use standard tools wherever possible, which will also reduce training costs and make it much easier for you to bring in temporary staff when they are needed.

Careful thought should also be given to hardware selection. You need the right balance of high-capacity printers and personal printers. Your professionals will all be originating documents, reports, speeches and presentations. Linking them all to distant shared printers can cost more in frustration and time than it saves in hardware. Printer linking might cost more in upfront labour and hardware than the capital costs of a high-quality small laser printer.

When you buy independent workstations, specify them with your standard wordprocessor and database tools installed on the hard disk rather than taking them from a network. Having some low-cost, easily portable hardware will give you much more operational flexibility and security against failure of networks, and will also reduce the networking costs when you move people around.

You should also watch the way you buy and service your fax machines and photocopiers. Subject to your employer's rules, you need to consider when to buy and when to lease and what service arrangements to put in place. All these costs can vary enormously and create a long-term budget problem if they are mismanaged. You must put clear control mechanisms in place to avoid this. Read the small print in all equipment lease and service contracts.

Media and other monitoring services can also run away with money. Ironically, your budget planning might be knocked off course by the costs of monitoring particularly successful media relations initiatives. All the agencies you use for this type of work need a written brief which includes clear guidance on cost control. For example, it is better to get broadcast monitoring services to call you before they automatically provide expensive multiple copies of material which has appeared in a similar form on a number of radio stations.

DISTRIBUTION LISTS

You may use distribution agencies for sending material to standard contact lists such as the media, but rely on your own lists for items such as customer magazines and courtesy copies of the report and accounts.

Your own lists will probably consist of two different types of contacts. They will include your prime targets to whom you mail material unless you have been specifically requested not to do so. The lists are likely to include many other recipients who requested courtesy copies in the past but who may not be of any long-term benefit to you.

Prune your lists regularly by including a repeat order form with the publication so that these casual recipients have to confirm their continued interest. You could also take the opportunity to obtain feedback about the publication and its readership by building a questionnaire into the repeat request form.

MARKET AND OPINION RESEARCH

Using research to monitor attitudes towards your organisation is vital but this can consume a large part of your budget. The use of collaborative tracking studies, where the same audience is researched in one survey on behalf of a number of companies, is a valuable tool. It enables you to buy much more coverage of your audiences than you could afford by yourself.

In addition to studies covering specific groups such as shareholders and politicians, there are omnibus studies through which you can put several questions to a large sample of the general public for a modest cost.

SPONSORSHIP AND CORPORATE HOSPITALITY

Much money is wasted on sponsorship and you should examine all such activity to ensure that it is targeted to important audiences and that it positions your company in an appropriate way. You may inherit sponsorship programmes which are more closely related to your chairperson's particular interests than to those of your target audiences. These situations need delicate management and one approach might be to enlist the support of other senior managers in raising the issues.

Whether it is associated with sponsorship or not, corporate

hospitality can be expensive, and organisations sometimes repeat traditional events year after year so that the impact on guests is limited. It pays to freshen up your corporate events from time to time by looking for new, lower-cost ideas. Doing simple things well is a sound philosophy which can save a lot of cash.

CONSULTANCY COSTS

You will want to get the best possible value from the money you spend on consultancies (Chapter 14 looks at the different ways of paying them). The time input system, where you pay for whatever hours the job takes, requires the most rigorous controls to avoid unpleasant budget surprises. One alternative is to agree a small retainer to finance a basic agreed programme and then to top this up later with project work at agreed fees.

Almost all forms of consultancy remuneration involve an assessment of hours worked, for that is the prime asset the consultancy has to sell you. Therefore it pays to conserve the time of your consultants. Start meetings on time, keep them short and avoid having more of the account team present than you really need. Hold discussions and get work carried out at the most junior level in the consultancy at which it will be effective. The managing director's hourly charge might be three times that of an account executive.

Remember that one way or another you are paying for travel time, telephone time and possibly even the time you spend at lunch with your consultants. This is not because consultancies are grasping but is a reflection of the fact that expert time is what they sell. When it is necessary for the account team to travel extensively on your behalf you should check and agree the time and personal expense implications.

The consultancies will charge you for their necessary office costs such as telephones, photocopying, messengers, and so on. Bear in mind that you will probably be paying the fully absorbed marked-up cost of these incidentals. Take as much of this administration in house as you can and agree the basis for charges or you may be surprised by the size of the bill.

The consultancy you use may make large external purchases on your behalf, such as print design and production or exhibition materials. Your contract will state the basis on which the invoices for these projects will be treated. The management and handling charge might be an additional 17.65 per cent, which equates to 15 per cent of the gross billing. You pay this charge to remunerate the consultancy for the costs of handling the invoice through its financial systems and for its management of the project. Often it is preferable to have the costs billed without mark-up directly to your own organisation by the supplier. You would then agree a management fee for the work the consultancy carries out on the project or cover it within the retainer.

The same principle applies to the costs of distributing news releases and other materials via the specialist services for this purpose. You might find it more beneficial to negotiate with these services and get them to invoice you directly.

COST-EFFECTIVE CREATIVE PROGRAMMES

Creative design and production projects are a big item in most departmental budgets. They include activities as varied as the production of company brochures, exhibition stands and audio-visual programmes. There are many opportunities for saving money, provided you are prepared to shop around and to link your materials together in a matrix structure (see below).

Selecting creative suppliers

There is an enormous range of suppliers, as demonstrated by the number of cold sales calls and mailshots you will receive. It is useful to have several approved suppliers in each area of creative production enabling you to get the benefits that come from a lasting relationship without losing price competitiveness. Several of your regular suppliers can be asked to compete for each project. Occasionally, you should also give opportunities to new suppliers by widening the pitch list beyond your normal circle.

It is necessary to have an open mind in order to buy well. Some of the larger and best-known creative agencies can be competitive on smaller jobs if they are given a clear brief. This is particularly true if they want to get your organisation on their client list for prestige purposes. At the same time there are small, low-cost operations which are capable of producing work of a high creative quality and providing outstanding personal service on a very small budget.

Sometimes the use of a freelance designer or creative director in combination with an efficient low-cost production house will give you the ideal combination of creativity and cost control.

Adopting a matrix approach

Planning your creative materials within a design and production matrix will strengthen your corporate identity as well as saving money. Take a broad look at your organisation's total needs for brochures, audiovisual programmes and display materials. Commission your supplier to design a comprehensive concept into which all your productions can be slotted as budgets become available. Plan all the items so that they complement each other in terms of creativity and message delivery. Make sure that in the design contract you protect your ability to implement the production through other suppliers.

Adopting this method will involve slightly higher upfront costs but will save a great deal of time later and reduce the cost of subsequent productions. It will also strengthen your corporate identity by presenting a consistent visual image to your audiences.

For example, your subsidiary companies or operating divisions may need their own brochures. The creative style for these, including cover design, typography, page layout and references to the parent organisation, can be designed as one project, matching your corporate brochure. Individual brochures are then produced as the need arises.

If your organisation needs several video programmes, plan a matrix for these and maximise the use of the creative concepts and production work such as script writing and filming. When you make your own corporate video, check with your colleagues to find out what other programmes may be required in the future so that any opportunities to shoot appropriate footage are taken. You might include in the brief for the video the simultaneous production of short modules from the programme. These could be used on exhibition stands, for positioning the group within subsidiary programmes or as mood setters for opening your management meetings and conferences.

Adopt a standard style for all 35mm slides and computer-produced presentation visuals. This should cover typography, colours and layout. Standardisation will enable you to mix and match slides from different presentations, improving visual consistency and saving origination costs.

The matrix principle can be applied to much more of your creative material, including exhibition displays, advertising and the text for brochures and news releases. It will extract maximum value from your investment of time and money in the creative area.

COST-EFFECTIVENESS IS HEROIC

Give priority to cost-effectiveness and, with the support of your team, you will find many other ways of delivering value for money. Success in public relations work will win recognition for your department, but achieving it on a small budget could make heroes of you.

8

Creating your team

ASSESSING THE RESOURCE REQUIRED

If you are creating or reconstructing a department you should start by assessing the size of team you need – the number of people and at what levels. You will need a balance between strategic planning, implementation and support skills. The type of experience and specialisation required will have to be considered.

You need to consider the ideal age profile to provide a satisfactory balance in the team and to take account of career development and succession planning for the future.

Factors in structuring your team
- size and scope of tasks
- specialisation and experience
- succession planning
- internal/external resource balance
- level of strategic input versus implementation

All these factors will be influenced by the nature of the organisation and driven by the responsibilities and goals of the department. A busy team is a happy team if it is well managed so, financial considerations apart, you should avoid over-staffing. It will probably be most cost effective to use external consultants to fill the gaps if you cannot smooth the workload. You will need to consider the other reasons for utilising external consultants. For example, if you need a specialist skill but cannot justify a full-time staff appointment, it will be sensible to hire this capability from a consultancy.

Some managers look for sector experience or an existing contact base when recruiting staff. These provide useful bonuses. However, it is more important to choose the highest-quality individual with the right balance of skills. Public relations capability, like finance or human resource, is a transferable skill and practitioners should be able to adapt to any sector. Contacts can soon be built up by the right person.

GENERALISTS OR SPECIALISTS?

You will need to decide whether to recruit and structure your team around practitioners with general or specialist skills and experience. You might need to recruit a specialist by area of public relations such as investor relations or government affairs. Alternatively, there might be a requirement for specialists in particular techniques such as media relations or sponsorship.

There is no point in having a team of strategic public relations planners if there is nobody who can write a news release or prepare a brief for a video production. Equally, there is no value in having a brilliant implementation team if there is nobody to write a strategy and a programme.

Your approach to all these issues will depend on your areas of activity and the size and nature of your tasks. These factors will govern the way you structure your department's operations. Some managers do this by audience with people concentrating on financial communication, government affairs, and so on. Other departments are structured by techniques with team members who are responsible perhaps for looking after creative services, media relations or events management. It is important to consider your internal clients. You may be dealing with a simple monolithic organisation or you may be working for an employer with lots of subsidiaries or regional operations. In these cases there can be great benefit in designating your team members as 'account managers' for specific internal clients in addition to their corporate roles.

There is no right or wrong answer to these questions, but they all have to be considered before you choose an approach which matches your tasks and the people you have or can recruit. Whatever you do should take full account of the need to provide job satisfaction and career development for your team. Figures 8.1, 8.2 and 8.3 are examples of structures for different types of organisation.

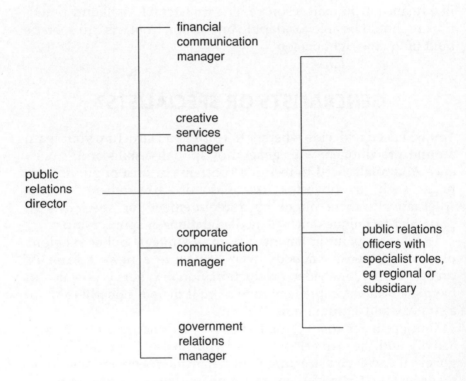

Figure 8.1 *Possible outline structure for a corporate department*

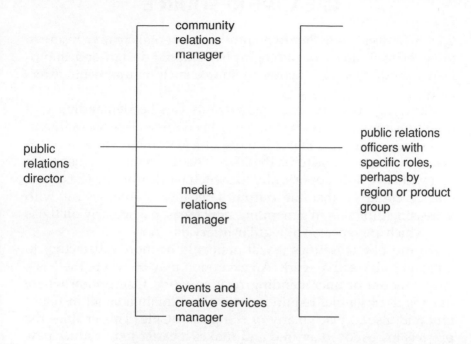

Figure 8.2 *Possible outline structure for a subsidiary or other national body with broad public contact*

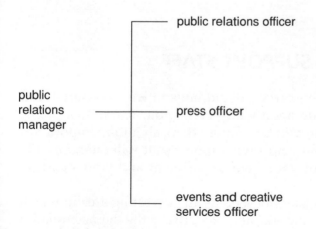

Figure 8.3 *Possible outline structure for a major regional entity with public involvement*

CREATIVE RESOURCE

You must decide whether to maintain an internal creative resource to cover such areas as photography, graphic design and audiovisual production or whether to source such requirements externally.

Managing creative production teams can be demanding and time consuming. It may be that your need for such services fluctuates significantly and that it is more efficient to buy these services externally. Another factor is that if you have a small in-house team you will have little opportunity to switch work around. The consequence could be that the output falls into a creative rut with increasing difficulty in generating new ideas, particularly on those jobs which are repeated at regular intervals.

For most organisations it will generally be more satisfactory to outsource all creative work. An exception may be where there is a large amount of undemanding routine work. One option where there is a substantial requirement is to maintain a small in-house unit and also to place many of the jobs outside. This enables the projects to be moved around and makes it easier to introduce new ideas.

However you commission creative work you should ensure that you have up-to-date legal advice on copyright issues. You should take all possible steps to secure for your employers the copyright and all other legal rights to the creative ideas and materials you utilise.

SUPPORT STAFF

The support staff who carry out administrative, secretarial and other functions for you are a vital part of your team. As a public relations manager you will be telling others about the importance of first impressions. So your own support staff will often provide the first impression of your own department and your management style.

Public relations is generally seen as an interesting area in which to work, so you should be able to attract the highest-quality support staff. Bear in mind that there are some very able people around who, because of family commitments, are unwilling to work full time. A part-time administrator who can vary their work days and hours to meet particular work requirements can provide you with a flexible resource.

You should value and develop your support staff. Make sure that they are fully aware of your overall aims and programme and encourage them to take as much responsibility as they can handle. In this way their own careers will be more interesting and you and your qualified professionals in turn will be more able to push yourselves to higher levels of achievement.

Typical outlines for job descriptions of professional team members

Public relations director

- Develops and supports internal and external communication worldwide.
- Contributes to group management process as top team member.
- Develops a long-term public relations strategy for the organisation, covering all key audiences in an integrated approach.
- Establishes policies and procedures to ensure strategy is implemented effectively and consistently.
- Presents an annual action plan and budget.
- Creates, leads and manages an effective public relations team.

Corporate communication manager

- Acts as deputy to the public relations director in all areas.
- Takes lead responsibility for group internal communication programmes.
- Manages the department's support to business divisions through group marketing communication and community relations programmes.
- Coordinates all media relations activities at group and divisional level.
- Manages the department's administration and operating procedures.

Government relations manager

- Develops a worldwide matrix of all elected representatives and public officials with a potential interest in the organisation.

- Plans contact programmes designed to build relationships with the above.
- Monitors issues within the organisation which may create public concern or require governmental support; recommends and implements action programmes to address these.
- Maintains a database of all public sector contacts made throughout the organisation.
- Monitors the policy debate within all governmental bodies to identify issues which may become relevant to the business in the future.

Creative services manager

- Manages the group corporate identity and ensures that appropriate visual standards are established and maintained through an operating manual.
- Manages production of corporate publications, including the report and accounts, corporate brochure and other group publications.
- Produces a range of audiovisual material to meet all group presentation needs.
- Manages group advertising.
- Produces all other creative materials needed at group level including display material and promotional merchandise.
- Ensures that a high-quality library of essential photography is created and maintained.
- Takes overall responsibility for the creative quality and cost-effectiveness of all departmental output and for monitoring creative standards throughout the organisation.

General public relations manager or officer working at divisional or site level

- Identifies the operation's public relations needs and develops strategies and action plans for approval by the general manager.
- Takes responsibility for divisional internal communication, marketing communication support programmes and community relations.
- Supports group programmes with other key audiences as required.

- Ensures that the division's activities are properly represented in group communications.
- Liaises with the corporate communication team so that activities are supportive of group policies.

RECRUITMENT AND SELECTION

Research has shown that public relations is viewed by students as one of the most attractive career options. You must be careful, therefore, about the methods of recruitment you use or you will be deluged with applicants unqualified by experience or education who believe that they can 'get on well with people'.

Key steps in recruitment process
- prepare a written brief
- involve your personnel officer
- consider recruitment consultancy
- advertise selectively
- allow two to six months

Recruitment is a time-consuming process and you will need help. Only the most senior public relations appointments will be of interest to the general management recruitment companies, so you are unlikely to involve them. However, a number of recruitment consultancies specialising in the public relations area offer a range of services from 'head hunting' through searching their existing databases of possible candidates to managing a recruitment advertisement and handling the response for you. Using their services should reduce your own workload significantly.

You should be highly selective about the media you choose for recruitment advertising. *PR Week* is the starting point for UK recruitment, perhaps supplemented by insertions in national or regional newspapers. Please see below an example of a job advertisement for a divisional public relations officer followed by comments on the example advertisement.

Public Relations Officer

FINECO CHEMICAL DIVISION

Fineco, the international manufacturing group, requires a public relations officer to plan and implement integrated communication programmes for its chemical division.

Based at the chemicals division headquarters in Bleaktown, close to the Blankshire Wold and its attractive coastal resorts, the public relations officer will report to the divisional managing director and will also work closely with the Fineco corporate communication team in London.

The main responsibilities will include internal communication, community relations and public relations support to the marketing team.

Candidates must be holders of a professional qualification approved by the Institute of Public Relations and be able to demonstrate enthusiasm, creativity and the potential to build a career in a successful worldwide group.

The initial salary will be around £XX,000 and a car will be provided along with other large company benefits.

Apply to Jean Jones, title, address, enclosing a full CV and details of current salary.

- This advertiser is carefully deterring the 'get on well with people' but unqualified candidates.
- The tone of the ad is designed to avoid over-glamourising the job.
- There is a specific requirement for a public relations qualification.
- Fineco is careful to avoid sexism, ageism and other prejudices.
- There is nothing in the ad to deter a newly qualified candidate.
- The salary level stated will give some indication of seniority but it is best to leave some flexibility here if possible.

- If a car is definitely available this can be a major attraction to candidates but it is sometimes better to leave this as an incentive to be offered later.
- The international references, the team involvement at group level and the hint of career development should all be attractive to ambitious candidates.
- Fineco is clearly concerned about the image of Bleaktown with those who do not know the area so is taking care to refer to its surrounding attractions.

You will need to work closely with your colleagues in the personnel function in selecting and appointing your team. They will bring their own wide specialist knowledge and experience in recruitment, cover the legal aspects for you and ensure that you comply with your organisation's procedures.

It will be helpful if you can arrange for one particular personnel officer to cover all your recruitment and ongoing personnel needs. He or she will become a valuable part of your extended team, providing you with expertise and counsel on all aspects of personnel motivation and development.

Before beginning the selection process you should produce a written brief outlining the qualifications, skills, experience and characteristics you require. You and your advisers will then assess the candidates against these criteria and draw up an initial shortlist for interview. Make sure that your programme of initial interviews, appraisal and final interview is designed to give you enough information and the time to form an opinion about your preferred candidates. Bad appointments are expensive and difficult to reverse. Your appointee will be a representative of your organisation and it is likely that your chief executive or whoever you report to will want to meet them before a final offer is made. Bear in mind that it usually takes longer to finalise an appointment than you expect – perhaps two to six months depending on the notice period required.

QUALIFICATIONS

In planning recruitment you will be identifying the experience which the candidates need to fulfil your requirements. In addition, you will want to assess the formal qualifications which you require.

Until the late 1980s and 1990s the UK lagged behind many other countries in formal higher education for public relations. The IPR now has its own diploma that covers the strategic roles and functions of the public relations practitioner. It provides knowledge and understanding of the theory and practice needed to develop as an effective professional.

With the creation of a range of first-degree and postgraduate courses, many other options are available. Those recognised by the IPR as leading to full membership have been evaluated against the industry's educational matrix which defines the knowledge required to practise public relations.

Arguably the most valuable courses from an employer's point of view are those which combine the theory of public relations practice with general management skills and a strong element of practical experience, perhaps through a year out with an employer. Another favoured route is a relevant first degree such as politics or psychology, supplemented by an intensive postgraduate qualification.

The movement towards vocational qualification has been reinforced by the launch of formal national vocational qualifications in the UK.

Candidates with recognised qualifications have a flying start and achieve much more and more quickly than the beginners of the past with no foundation other than aptitude. Information about approved qualifications is available from the IPR which produces detailed literature on the subject.

There are opportunities to take students from some of the approved courses into your department for periods varying from two weeks to a year. This can be a valuable method of identifying potential candidates for future appointments. There is no better way of assessing capability, potential and the fit with your existing team.

Another approach is to build a long-term relationship with one of the approved courses, providing career advice to the students, course materials and project assignments. In this way you will give valuable support to the development of young professionals and at the same time identify talent for the future.

If you are considering older candidates it is much less likely that they will have a formal qualification than their young counterparts, in which case you will have to assess the knowledge, experience, and personal and professional development of the candidate even more thoroughly through the interview and assessment process. With any candidate you will always have the option of encouraging or requiring them to obtain additional formal qualification after their appointment.

The public relations business is steadily advancing towards higher levels of formal qualification and it can be important for you to demonstrate to colleagues in other functions that the role does require an extensive base of theoretical, technical and practical knowledge.

RECRUITING SUPPORT STAFF

Your support team of administrators and secretaries will be important representatives both internally and externally. There is a great deal of routine administration in any public relations department and this needs to be handled effectively.

Recruitment of support staff requires as much care, therefore, as you give to selecting your professional team. You will need to define the jobs carefully as otherwise you may attract candidates who assume that public relations work is mainly about entertainment and photographic shoots.

In London and other large cities secretarial recruitment agencies have developed a specialist knowledge of the needs of the sector. It is well worth considering using such an agency if this is possible. Otherwise you will need to use a general agency, which should be given a clear written briefing on your requirements.

Another approach is to place a carefully worded advertisement in the local media and to enlist the help of your personnel officer to assess the responses.

Many of the key aptitudes for public relations work apply equally to your support staff. Accuracy of work output is most important as the results are so often on public view. Reliability, flexibility and a real interest in the organisation and their own role within it are vital attributes.

INDUCTION PROGRAMMES FOR NEW RECRUITS

Anyone working in public relations needs to gain a rapid familiarity with the organisation because of their immediate involvement in handling enquiries. It is therefore essential to arrange induction programmes that are appropriate to the past experience and new work responsibilities of your recruits.

Induction should involve briefing on the company's strategies, philosophy and structure. It should cover business activities, markets, products, services and customers. Information needs to be provided about the key people in the organisation and also on the particular individuals with whom the new employee will have regular contact.

Depending on the role of the recruit, induction can include personal briefings from colleagues in the department, reading documents and watching company audiovisuals with an opportunity for discussion. Production demonstrations and site visits will be essential for anyone with a significant communication responsibility. New administrative staff may need to be sent on the introduction to public relations courses which are available.

Most importantly, the programme must cover the department's responsibilities and procedures, with detailed exposure to the procedures manual.

APTITUDE FOR PUBLIC RELATIONS

Apart from experience and qualification, you should consider the personal characteristics, traits and aptitude needed to succeed in public relations.

Some key aptitudes for public relations
- personal communication skills
- imaginative and lateral thinker
- streetwise and worldly
- sensitive to widely different audiences
- sound judgement
- numerate
- well presented personally

Your candidates will need to be intelligent with flexible and agile minds. This will help them to deal with the variety of matters which pass through your department and which might range from the catastrophic to the bizarre. Your team do not all have to qualify for MENSA, but they will need to be streetwise and able to think laterally.

A sensitivity to the views and perspectives of widely differing groups, from manufacturing teams to investment fund managers, is a vital attribute. Messages will have to be correctly pitched for such diverse audiences. The public relations officer will have to predict to management how particular messages are likely to be received by people with very different backgrounds and interests and help to interpret the responses.

Sensitivity to other people's views should be accompanied by good judgement on how to deal with different people, perhaps in unexpected and difficult situations and often with very little time to react.

Your team will find these tasks easier if they are worldly and well read. They need to have good antennae, stimulated by a degree of curiosity.

If you want to build a team of future winners, they will need to be numerate, particularly if you are responsible for financial communication. In any case, they will need to be able to manage budgets and to understand the difference between being costly and being cost effective.

Your team will be visible representatives of your organisation, your department and yourself. They should be personable and well presented with a degree of presence and good personal communication skills.

Avoid compromises in creating your team, because the commitment you invest will pay big dividends in your future achievements.

9

Managing the team

DEVELOPING THE MEMBERS

The primary method of developing your team members is through the way you assign responsibility to them, supervise their work and delegate additional tasks as their skills improve. This 'on-the-job' development is, of course, one of the most important responsibilities you have towards the members of your team. The larger the department, the more your staff can help each other to refine their skills. You will encourage this by promoting a good team spirit within your operation.

You should assign clear accountabilities for specific areas to your staff, but you can also encourage them to work together in teams outside their personal responsibilities to handle specific assignments. This will develop them and bring fresh and varied ideas to your programmes.

Actions for professional development
● blending specialisation with variety
● forming *ad hoc* project teams
● appraisal and coaching
● contact with senior management

- international exposure
- external courses and qualifications
- networking with colleagues

Spreading the tasks and experience

We have already looked at alternative ways of structuring your department. Individuals might have responsibility for audiences such as government or financial, for techniques such as media relations, or for supporting particular line management teams on perhaps a subsidiary company or regional basis. Whichever structure suits you best, you can also ask individual team members to take responsibility for being the focus for your department's activities in some other area. For example, if you have a financial communications specialist you might ask this person to take additional responsibility for your audio-visual programmes. You can also ask team members to take on particular administrative responsibilities, maybe for budget monitoring or for the department's information technology requirements.

All these ideas can play an important part in developing and motivating your team. You can ring the changes by moving responsibilities around from time to time to keep people 'on their toes' and to stimulate fresh thinking.

Increasing exposure and contacts

You should ensure that all your team members feel comfortable in working with the organisation's senior management. Expose them gradually as their confidence builds. Be content if your general manager develops direct relationships with your subordinates and accept this as a sign of confidence in your selection and development of the team. Do make sure, however, that you are aware of the general content of all such communication.

If your organisation operates internationally, try to share some of the necessary overseas travel around those colleagues who are capable of operating at this level. It will develop them and motivate them at the same time. Avoid the temptation to invent trips just for this purpose, however, as this would damage seriously the credibility of your department.

Continuing professional development

You should encourage your team to pursue external development opportunities. Much benefit will result from participation in the IPR's continuing professional development programmes, including workshops, seminars and specialist group meetings. These now include structured programmes leading to Accredited Practitioner status. Apart from straightforward learning opportunities, there can be considerable value in making contacts with colleagues from other companies who may include your customers, suppliers, lenders or investors. Some of your team may be able to gain additional formal qualifications through part-time study courses, distance learning or national vocational qualifications.

APPRAISALS

It is almost certain that your employer will operate a formal system of personnel appraisal. If this is so, you should participate with enthusiasm as it will provide a structure for reviewing the performance of your team and discussing their aspirations and your own relationships. If there is no such system, you should attempt to persuade your organisation to introduce one. Meanwhile you can introduce a system of your own and follow it consistently from year to year.

Essential content of appraisal

- summary of responsibilities
- changes since last appraisal
- performance against previous objectives
- factors influencing performance
- future objectives for monitoring
- professional development since last appraisal
- future professional development plan
- future career potential

The personnel appraisal should normally take place annually and it will be supplemented by your own continuous appraisal of individual performance based on your programme and the personal action plans for your team members. It will be valuable if you can incorporate your personal action plans within the standard personnel appraisal programme used across your organisation.

The appraisal should include a summary of the jobholder's current responsibilities, noting any changes which have taken place during the previous year. You should formally record performance against the action plan objectives with a commentary on the factors which have influenced both successes and failures. The latter may have been outside the control of your team member.

You should also include a schedule of the jobholder's personal action responsibilities within the total departmental plan for the following year.

Appraisal should also include an annual review of the training and professional development needs of your staff and a chance for them to state their own hopes for the future and current concerns.

Example of an annual professional development and training plan for a public relations officer

Extension of working experience

- Act as personal assistant to the public relations director on the annual financial results announcement.
- Visit the operations in France and write a profile for the internal magazine.
- Act as secretary to the company working group planning the 50th anniversary events.

Company training

- Attend the group-wide graduate development course.
- Attend the company training seminar on finance for non-financial executives.
- Attend the IT department's MS Word advanced course.

Specialist functional training

- Participate in IPR financial communication workshop.
- Join the IPR City and Financial Group as an active member.
- Visit the company's stockbrokers and merchant bank.

High-quality managers will find the annual personnel appraisals relatively straightforward as they will already be alert to the issues through their regular communication with the team.

Perhaps the most satisfactory process for both parties is for the manager and the team member to complete separate drafts of the appraisal form before meeting to compare views. Appraisal is a two-way process and an opportunity for both parties to review and improve their operating relationship. Both parties should agree and sign the final version of the appraisal document.

REMUNERATION AND EXPENSES

Very wide differences exist in the market salaries for public relations staff according to location, sector and experience. These differences partly reflect the general approach of the organisation but are sometimes influenced by its view of the value of public relations work.

Sometimes it is possible to get people to work for you at a lower salary than the market rate in order to gain particular experience or because they are getting exceptional job satisfaction. In the end, however, you will need to pay the market rate if you wish to recruit and retain the people you need.

Paying the market rate

You will need to have a good understanding of what the market rates for salaries and benefits actually are. You can obtain this by following recruitment advertisements, talking to recruitment consultants and asking colleagues in other organisations. There may be published salary studies which are of some help. Those which rely on people filling in survey forms can be distorted because of the tendency for the more senior professionals to ignore them.

If your organisation is exceptionally mean with fringe benefits, you are unlikely to be able to change the policy, so you may have to compensate for this with a higher basic salary. Apart from external comparisons, you will need to ensure that your team is treated fairly in comparison with their colleagues in other functions in your organisation. Young public relations professionals, for example, should be paid at least as well as young lawyers, accountants or engineers. Your case will be strengthened if you employ young professionals with a recognised qualification.

The variances in salary and benefits become enormous at the

more senior levels in public relations. The head of the function in a large public company will be remunerated within the top management group in the company, which includes the personnel director, corporate development director and the marketing director if this position exists at group level. The chief executive of a large consultancy may be paid more than your own chief executive.

Watching the level of expense claims

Reimbursement of the out-of-pocket expenses of your team should not cause any problems if you have selected them well and made the rules clear. There is little need for excessive entertainment in public relations work, despite the myths about this. However, those myths may mean that others in your organisation keep a watchful eye on your team's expenses.

It is likely, however, that your team will have larger expense claims than many of their colleagues in other departments. There are certain types of expenditure which are specific to public relations. These include such items as telephone calls made from home, mobile telephones and the purchase of newspapers and magazines. Make sure that your policy on such items is clearly understood and applied fairly and consistently. Be aware of the current rules applied by the tax authorities on reimbursable expenses and inform your team accordingly.

Discourage your team from accepting excessive entertainment from suppliers and ensure that they understand what you consider to be acceptable. If you need to have occasional working lunches with suppliers, pick up the modest bill yourselves sometimes. Apart from creating goodwill, it will send messages about your approach to your commercial relationship.

TITLES

There is no standard approach to nomenclature in public relations, and this often causes confusion. In some organisations the title 'public affairs manager' may be used for the person who heads up a general public relations department. In other cases, this title may be reserved for the person who is responsible for government relations or issues management.

For the first-level professional, capable of giving strategic advice, titles such as public relations officer or corporate commu-nication officer are frequently used. Some organisations use a title such as public relations adviser to denote an advisory capability.

Public relations executive or communication executive can be useful titles as they mirror the terminology used in public relations consultancies.

The structure of titles you adopt has to position your team correctly in the relationships they manage externally, as well as sending the right signals to their internal contacts.

MANAGEMENT STYLE

The success of your department will be based on the team you put together and the processes you put in place to ensure that it has purpose, motivation and organisation. The extra ingredient which will make the difference between good performance and outstanding achievement is your own personal style of manage-ment.

Develop and refine your own leadership skills and be sensitive to the response you induce from your team. The most important factor to achieve success will be good communication. Your own operation should be an example to the rest of the organisation of the added value which comes from exceptionally good internal communication.

The precise way in which you communicate with your team will depend on the number of members involved and whether they are all in one location or spread around the organisation. In any event, ensure that every department member attends a regular team briefing. In a small operation this may be a meeting of the whole department. In a larger department you may want to have regular section meetings, supplemented by occasional meetings of the whole department together, if the location permits.

Managing your team meetings

There are several objectives for your team meetings. You will want to ensure that everyone is well briefed on the progress of the organisation to which you belong. You should also cover the most recent work of the team, highlighting collective achievements and reviewing any problems which have occurred. This will give staff an opportunity to make suggestions for improving the way you operate. You will also look at the future work programme, highlighting priorities and hearing any ideas or concerns about the way the plans will be implemented.

Typical team meeting agenda

- review major developments in the organisation
- status of action minutes from previous meetings
- budget report and forecast
- review key issues in team monthly reports
- status update on departmental action plans
- open agenda section for items from the team
- major projects in the next month

It is also vital to have an open agenda to which anyone can contribute items for discussion or questions they wish to have answered. Make sure that your team understands that you are interested in any issues which concern them, however trivial they may seem. Give people an opportunity to put items on the agenda without their names being attached in case there is any embarrassment or nervousness. If certain issues are not raised, use your closest colleagues to find out why. Be sensitive to concerns and anticipate the questions by raising them yourself. An open management style in which issues are faced will lead to better performance and a happier team.

If you are a natural leader, your skills will bring out the best in your team. If you have doubts about your leadership skills, seek help and advice from your manager and from your personnel colleagues.

Leadership, communication and teamwork are vital factors in delivering achievement and job satisfaction, however tough the tasks may be.

10

Managing internal relationships

REPORTING UPWARDS

Your own manager could be another public relations professional or a general manager. If you do report to a public relations manager, you should have been given a clear understanding by your boss as to how your relationship should be managed. This will cover the areas where you have authority to act and those where consultation is required. You should be able to expect that your contribution is understood and properly valued by the general manager to whom the function reports ultimately. Your own development will be helped by access to general management. Good teamwork will result if you keep your own manager informed of the subjects which you are discussing at this higher level.

'Dotted-line' relationships

If you are part of a larger public relations operation, you are likely to be managing a specialised section, subsidiary or regional operation, in which case, you will have an operational reporting relationship with the head of the activity you are supporting. Such 'dotted-line' relationships can need careful management. You will need to recognise the operating managers' role and status while guiding them within the public relations area and keeping your functional manager informed. If the dotted and solid lines on the organisation chart are drawn the other way around, you will have the converse task of operating independently of the centre within defined areas but responding to corporate procedures and aspirations.

Operating at chief executive level

If you hold the most senior public relations job in the organisation, you should be reporting to the chief executive or chairman. You may be able to make a judgement about their operating style, but it is best to ask formally how they want you to conduct your side of the relationship. Establish the type of issues they want to hear about and the decisions on which consultation is required. Clarify what kind of regular formal reporting is expected.

You will need to establish a routine for gaining access, for it is impossible to perform well in public relations without this. There will be urgent issues which require rapid access and decisions, such as whether to respond to a stock market development or to appear on television that day. There will be other matters which can be put on one side for another day. Hopefully, your boss will have a regular 'folder' meeting with you at which a whole series of such items can be dealt with efficiently. Where you need a major review, perhaps of a budget or a results presentation, it is best to schedule a special meeting. Apart from all this, there are more trivial issues on which you might need a quick decision in order to progress your workload. Your best ally in this and in the broader question of access is your manager's personal assistant or secretary. The person in this job can make your life so much easier by getting you through the door or clearing the minor points for you in their daily round-up with the boss.

In building your role with the chief executive or chairperson, you should naturally become a close confidant or adviser. You should be seen as being detached and well informed with good networks of contacts. You must be prepared to be brave but not foolhardy in raising issues and passing on information and advice, sometimes on delicate and personal matters. If you can win trust in this role, you will be even more valuable to your boss and to the organisation.

RELATIONSHIPS WITH OTHER STAFF FUNCTIONS

You will have a number of working relationships with other staff functions in the organisation. In some cases this will involve the direct professional support they give to you in managing your department. In other situations you will be working together on public relations programmes directed at audiences in which they have an interest. Some aspects of this have already been discussed in the analysis of the various areas of public relations in Chapter 2. Figure 10.1 summarises the principal relationships and the text below goes into more detail.

Finance

We have already looked at the involvement you will have with the finance department with regard to the management of your budget and the importance of handling this in a disciplined way. If your organisation has a financial communication requirement, you will work closely with the finance department on those programmes. The report and accounts will probably be produced in partnership. You will also plan together the communication programmes for analysts and investors.

Occasionally, you may come across companies with a background of organisational politics. The financial communications area can be an arena for turf battles between the various departments which are involved. It is best if the parties can work together as a team, but if there are problems you will need to clarify accountabilities as the finance director is likely to bat higher in the organisation than the public relations director. Much of the information you need in order to carry out financial public relations will emanate from the finance function. It is as well to formalise your access to this information through the receipt of board reports, management accounts and other papers.

Figure 10.1 *Principal relationships with other staff functions*

Company secretary and legal section

The company secretary's department and legal section will be vital reference points for a number of issues. The company secretary is responsible for the agenda and minutes for the board and its committees. The department will know almost everything that is happening in the organisation. They will be a repository for vast amounts of knowledge about its history and detailed activities. A good company secretary will be one of your most valuable sources of information and advice.

Human resource

The personnel or human resources department will support you in managing your own team. You will also need to work closely with them in the organisation of internal communication. The statutory aspects of internal communication become ever more complex and the personnel staff should have the specialist expertise in this field. Cooperation in devising management development initiatives to improve the communication skills throughout the organisation will be vital. In multi-site organisations with a large workforce, there may be site personnel officers who can be useful for making sure that your programmes and materials are reaching the employee audience. They may also be of help to you in local community public relations activity.

Corporate planning

The corporate planning department will be able to give you a valuable insight into the strategic direction of the organisation. They will analyse the options for change and growth as well as the strategic threats which may emerge. The department will hold information in depth about markets, competitors, potential predators, economic trends and all the other factors which are relevant to your employer. They can provide considerable background material for speeches, the annual report and other communication vehicles.

Marketing

In Chapter 2 we examined the interface between the public relations and marketing functions and programmes. In a conglomerate company it is likely that the marketing function will be carried out at subsidiary level while public relations will be a corporate function. The respective roles must be clearly defined to avoid the territorial battles which can be a time-wasting irritant.

CONTROLLING AND INFLUENCING DOWNSTREAM PUBLIC RELATIONS ACTIVITIES

Depending on the nature of your organisation, you are likely to have an operating relationship with the management of subsidiary companies and of national or regional offices. They will have their own public relations needs as well as an involvement in your central programmes. You will need to agree what public relations resource they require and to help them to establish it. This may be through employing their own public relations team or it may be by using a consultancy. It is also possible that you have the proximity and the central resource to fulfil these needs yourself.

SUBSIDIARY PUBLIC RELATIONS TEAMS

If subsidiary public relations staff report to you, they will be part of your team and look to you for the leadership, communication and organisation referred to in Chapter 9. They should treat the general managers they serve almost as if they were their bosses without losing control of vital corporate issues. If they report to the general manager with a 'dotted line' to you, they will need to have a clear understanding of corporate policy and those areas which are delegated and those which need central approval. Even though these practitioners do not report to you, it is still your responsibility to provide professional development and leadership on a functional basis.

WORKING WITH SUBSIDIARY MANAGEMENT

The way in which you are viewed by the subsidiary general managers will be influenced by the culture and history of the organisation, the professionalism of your department, and the nature of the previous and current corporate involvement in subsidiary matters. You may be seen as a potential ally and a resource to be utilised. Alternatively, your starting point may be the perception of you as an expensive overhead of no real value. You could even be treated with caution as a vehicle by which the chief executive is pursuing change or even as a potential head office spy. It is sometimes said by profit centre managers that one of the world's great lies is the statement 'I'm from head office – I'm here to help'!

Despite this, you should aim to create a relationship in which you are a useful sounding board for subsidiaries on what might be acceptable to central management. In widespread operations your visits can deliver a helpful flavour of what is happening at the centre and why. It need hardly be said that you should avoid sitting in a head office ivory tower, and get out and about around the operations.

Balancing support and control

The balance between supporting subsidiary activity and achieving the necessary control is a delicate task and can be most difficult to achieve. You may not always be popular, but you can ensure that you are professional. In this process there are minimum operating standards which you need to have agreed in order to formalise your influence in the organisation.

Influencing appointments

You should insist on having a role in all appointments of public relations practitioners whether or not they are directly responsible to you. You should then take a hand in their professional development and career progression, including appraisal and remuneration.

You will also want to have a major say in the appointment of any public relations consultancies by involving yourself in the brief, the pitch list, the presentation and the monitoring of performance.

The public relations manual

A well-produced public relations operating manual is one of the most effective ways of communicating your strategies and management approach throughout your organisation. This is discussed in some detail in the next chapter.

Functional reviews

You should also expect to take part in regular management reviews of downstream public relations work. These will range from informal discussions during your regular visits through to formal functional reviews of the annual plan and budget.

COORDINATION CREATES ADDED VALUE

You may find that the total expenditure on subsidiary public relations is considerably more than your own central budget. It needs to be managed cost effectively and the programmes coordinated with your own, in order to create maximum impact and a consistent reputation. Unless separate trading names are involved, your audiences will not differentiate between the activities of subsidiary operations and the corporate body.

Working closely with subsidiary management will limit the possibility of damaging errors and create added value through a coordinated approach.

11

The public relations manual

Production of a public relations operating manual for your organisation is one of the most efficient ways of increasing the quality and consistency of the organisation's communication.

You can be certain that there is a financial operating manual which is probably treated with a degree of reverence by profit centre managers. You should aim to establish the same status for your public relations manual. Call it a communication manual if you prefer, for your management colleagues may recognise this title more readily as referring to a responsibility they hold.

THE PURPOSE OF THE MANUAL

The manual has a totally different role from that of your own departmental office procedures manual which is referred to in Chapter 13. It is additional to the corporate identity or visual standards manual already referred to. However, the visual standards manual could be included within it or at least produced in a matching format with cross-referencing.

Purpose of the public relations manual

- describes group public relations policies and structures
- explains what managers are encouraged to do and when they must check with the centre
- provides ideas and advice for managers on their own public relations programmes
- gives contact details for the public relations team for accessing help

Your public relations manual will be a source of ideas, help and encouragement to the managers around the organisation as they plan public relations activities within their operations. It will also be a control mechanism which states clearly the areas where public relations activity needs to be cleared with the centre. It will also set quality standards for the way in which public relations work is implemented throughout the organisation.

USERS OF THE PUBLIC RELATIONS MANUAL

The manual should be issued to all members of the management board, heads of group functions and all general managers. This list has to include the most senior manager at every location where public relations activity is being initiated.

Additional circulation will depend on the operating structure and the nature of the organisation. A natural cut-off point has to be defined so that the list can be administered and updates provided periodically. In practice, the list could number somewhere between 50 and 500 managers but there will be organisations which fall outside this range.

It is vital that a list of holders is created and maintained. This should be by job title and location and be included within the manual so that the structure of the list and the responsibility for onward communication and control is clear. It is also designed to demonstrate that the manual should stay with the position when the jobholder changes. It can be useful to number each copy.

When sites are closed or divested, the manual should be recovered. When sites are acquired, the holders' list should be amended and a manual issued as part of the acquisition or start-up process.

Typical contents list for a public relations manual

Introduction
Statement by chief executive.
Purpose and use of this manual.
List of holders.

Financial and Corporate Communication
Group policies.
Communicating with the financial community.
Crisis communication procedure.
Copyright policy.
Charitable donations and sponsorship.
Hospitality guidelines.

Government Relations
General group policies.
Company rules on political donations and involvement.
Communicating with legislators.

Marketing Communication
Group policies.
Coordinating communication with customers.
Group support activities.

Internal Communication
Group policies.
Communicating with employees – group support materials.
Ideas for site programmes.

Community Relations
Group policies.
Ideas for site programmes

Media Relations
Group policies.
Communicating with the media.
Implementing business and site programmes.

Corporate Identity
Group visual standards manual.
House style for written materials.

Appointing Consultants and Other Suppliers
Group policies on appointment of consultants.
Appointing other suppliers.
Producing briefs for consultants and suppliers.
List of approved suppliers.
Group policy on securing copyright.

Communication Support Materials
List of group publications.
Web site.
List of group audiovisual productions.
Promotional merchandise brochure.

Getting Help From The Centre
How group public relations can help.
List of group public relations contacts.

CONTENTS OF THE MANUAL

Every organisation has different requirements and no two public relations departments are structured in the same way. You will need to plan the contents of your own communication manual in relation to your particular situation, responsibilities and objectives. The example shown above is typical of the approach that might be adopted in a department with wide responsibilities in a major business.

You should set out the general policies in each area of communication with a clear statement of what is encouraged and which activities require your central involvement. The manual should explain how effective public relations can help to achieve business objectives. Include ideas for programmes, some basic advice on techniques and a clear statement of how to obtain specialist advice and support.

Include up-to-date lists of all the materials which are available from the centre and how your managers can access these. Your visual standards manual is likely to be a separate publication but there ought to be an explanation of its purpose and availability. You might also include at least the basic elements of the corporate identity with a sheet of logo bromides and colour references.

APPROVAL PROCESS

All policy statements in the manual should be circulated to the management board or similar body and be approved by the chief executive. This is done in order to achieve buy-in from the senior management group and to demonstrate to everyone else that the policies have their support and are mandatory.

One approach is to get the policies discussed and approved in manageable-size bites over a period of time and then to consolidate them into a manual when enough progress has been made. This will help to phase your own workload and make it easier to obtain real discussion and commitment than if you present the management group with a mass of material in one batch.

Any manual which you issue without going through a buy-in process of this kind may have little credibility with your colleagues. If there is controversy, your senior management might leave you high and dry with damage to your personal and departmental credibility.

LAUNCHING THE MANUAL

Give advance information to the recipients about the manual well before the launch. Explain the benefits of the project through your management briefing documents, at management conferences and by offering presentations to individual operations. This should help to prepare managers for the new tasks and restrictions you may be imposing, bringing objections to the concept into the public arena so that they can be addressed in advance.

The manual should be a living entity with future additions and updates. It is not essential to wait until all the contents are available to launch the project. The scope of the eventual contents could be covered in the index with some sections issued later. However, it would not be sensible to launch with less than half the contents complete.

The initial distribution should include a statement of endorsement from the chief executive with references to your department's responsibility for the management of the policies described in the manual.

PRODUCTION FORMAT

You could look at several alternative formats for a manual but a strong A4 size ring-binder has much in its favour. It is the usual format chosen for financial control manuals, is easy to update and will look sufficiently substantial.

Binders are readily available with clear plastic sleeves into which you can insert printed sheets on the front and back covers and in the spine. These should be attractively designed in your corporate identity.

In view of the relatively small circulation and the frequency of updates, it is practical and economic to produce the inside pages internally. A large stock of paper can be pre-printed externally with your logo and a distinctive design such as a box round the page edges to contain the copy. The text can then be produced on a personal computer and laser printed in house. The index and page numbering protocol needs to be designed to allow for future extensions.

KEEPING THE MANUAL ALIVE

You must ensure that the manual is not just a nine-day wonder but a living asset to your communication programmes. This will depend on meticulous attention to the circulation list and continual updating to make sure that the content remains fresh and relevant to the changing needs of the organisation.

You will achieve this by issuing new sections from time to time and by keeping the reference information, such as contact lists and schedules of publications, bang up to date. You should also include cross-references to the manual in your other management communications and seek feedback on its value when you visit the operations.

12

Managing external relationships

This book is about departmental management rather than management of public relations strategies and programmes. The aim of this chapter, therefore, is just to give some simple hints on the way you can approach managing external relationships within your department. Managing issues on behalf of your organisation is a wider subject addressed in another book in this series (*Public Relations in Practice*, Anne Gregory, ed., 1996).

RELATIONSHIPS WITH TARGET AUDIENCES

The public relations department will have extensive contacts with the target audiences within each of the distinct areas of public relations practice reviewed in Chapter 2 and summarised in Figure 12.1. Managing these contacts well is an essential element in the success of your programmes.

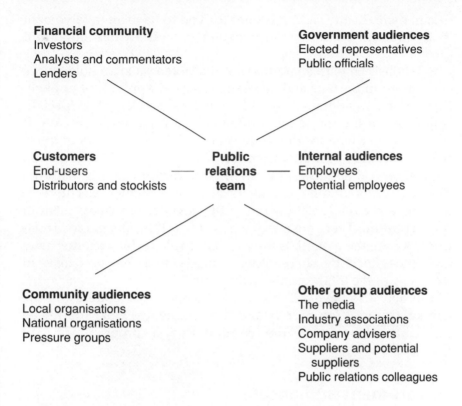

Figure 12.1 *Summary of important audiences*

The financial audience

In the area of financial communication for a public company you will need to agree lines of demarcation with the finance director and other colleagues. Specifically, the broker analysts must understand your role and what information they can obtain from you and what comes from the finance department. Sometimes there is a full-time investor relations officer in one department or the other. In other companies the finance director handles all primary financial information flows to analysts, but you might have a role in providing an extra contact point for confirming information already in the public arena. The key task is to make sure that the procedures are agreed and that the analysts do understand your role in them. In any case, it is vital for you to have an involvement in the quality of the communication process to this important group.

Relationships with shareholders and potential shareholders are even more important and similar principles apply. It is unlikely that the shareholder analyst will have the same degree of specialisation and desire for detailed financial information as a broker. It can work very well for the shareholders to have a variety of interfaces according to the situation. It might be appropriate for you to handle general enquiries, for the finance director to deal with the detailed needs of fund managers and for the chief executive to develop a personal relationship at the next tier of management in the institution. There are many ways of handling shareholder relations. Again, the essentials are that your role is defined internally and understood by shareholder contacts, and that you take an overview of the total communication process.

You may also have a direct role in contact with lenders and the general financial community and these audiences will certainly be recipients of some of the communication programmes you manage.

Government audiences

In the government relations arena it is likely that you will be a prime contact for elected representatives with an interest in your organisation. This may also apply to officials of national or local government. It will be your job to urge elected representatives to take a supportive interest in your organisation. Situations will also arise in which they will seek your support, perhaps on a community relations matter or the personal situation of a constituent who is an employee or supplier of your organisation.

You should have procedures for keeping representatives and officers informed of any of your activities which will affect their constituents or areas of interest. You should also have a working relationship with the officials in the government department which has a responsibility for your sector. All relationships should be conducted within the rules and the spirit of the guidelines covering the behaviour of elected representatives and officials. It is essential that your own approach to this sector is clearly defined in your departmental operating manual and available to anyone in the organisation who might be involved. The guidelines should include your organisation's rules about political contributions and other payments.

The customer audience

It is more difficult to define general principles for managing your relationships with customers. Your employer might have 50 customers or there could be 50 million. You might have a close involvement in marketing communication or simply be giving general advice within a total communication approach. Clearly, no organisation can exist without customers, although these might be differently defined in the public sector or in not-for-profit organisations. Your minimum position must be to ensure that you have a voice in the management of reputation with customers, as part of an integrated approach to managing the organisation's overall reputation. Any direct contact you have with customers must be professionally managed and properly communicated to your sales and marketing colleagues.

Internal audiences

The direct contact you have with employees will depend very much on their number and the spread of locations. In some cases your department could be a regular port of call for employees seeking information or advice. In other cases you may be just a source of last resort for direct contact, even if you are producing materials which are targeted at employees.

In all circumstances you will need to find methods of gaining a close understanding of the organisation's reputation with its employees as part of your overall communication responsibilities. The line managers have ultimate responsibility for communicating with their teams and you will want to hear their feedback. You can also make a point of talking to a cross-section of employees when you visit various locations. If there are formal channels for employee consultation, make sure that you participate.

Community audiences

Apart from these key target audiences there is a more diverse range of individuals and organisations to consider – local communities and community leaders in the areas where you operate, for example. You should clarify how these contacts are to be managed consistently between you and the location general managers. There is the whole range of lobby groups and individuals who believe that they have a legitimate interest in your affairs. Once they have identified you as a contact they can consume a great deal of time, so you will need to have a clearly defined policy for handling them.

Industry associations

It can be very worthwhile to involve yourself in industry bodies such as the Confederation of British Industry and in trade associations or other representative groups covering your activities. Here you can often find valuable sources of information or arrange for generic issues to be handled on an industry or sector basis. You will also meet your clients, competitors and suppliers and improve your knowledge of the sector and the way your own organisation is perceived. Generally you will find advantages from getting out and about and networking and it is difficult to be an effective and detached adviser internally unless you do this.

SALES CALLS

You are almost certain to be bombarded with letters and telephone calls from people who wish to sell you everything from consultancy services to directory entries and corporate hospitality. The telephone calls can be a particular nuisance and it is surprising how persistent and even irritating some salespeople can be. The best way of dealing with this problem is to have a simple rule that all such offers have to be put in writing. Your staff should explain briefly and firmly that it is company policy that purchase matters cannot be discussed on the telephone but that all letters will be considered.

COMPANY ADVISERS

You should establish direct working relationships with your organisation's professional advisers. These should include in particular stockbrokers, auditors, bankers and lawyers. You will find it useful to hear their views about the organisation's reputation, communications and policies. You may find that once they know and trust you they will be more relaxed with you than with those to whom they have a formal reporting relationship.

Having an open door to these advisers will be particularly valuable when your organisation is involved in a special situation such as a stock exchange listing or sponsorship of a parliamentary bill. You will find that the mutual understanding helps you to work together much better and they will see you as an asset and not try to cut you out of the process.

THE MEDIA

Good media relations are an important factor in most public relations programmes and deserve a book to themselves. Whatever message you have to manage, the result will be better if you handle the process well.

Vital factors in managing media relations
- availability around the clock
- maintain position papers
- prepare private Question and Answer briefs
- avoid jargon and extravagant claims
- short, factual news releases
- who? what? how? when? where? why?
- never expect to be 'off the record'
- return media calls immediately
- keep a note of all media calls
- provide access to management when needed
- understand the different media

Understand the media perception

Unfortunately, relations between public relations practitioners and journalists are not always good. There are two main reasons for this. One is that journalists are often on the receiving end of poor performance by unqualified or inexperienced practitioners. Puffy news releases are directed to the wrong journalists or publications.

Then the originator pesters the journalists about whether the release has been received, whether it will be used and whether they can be sent a clipping. The recipient may receive several hundred news releases each day and will become very angry about this type of approach which, sadly, does still happen. The press are much more likely to talk about such experiences than about the many good stories they run based on targeted and well-presented information from public relations teams.

The other factor which colours relations with the media is that many journalists equate public relations with media relations and assume that they are dealing with press officers with the sole responsibility of helping the media. The fact that you may only spend a small proportion of your time on media relations escapes them. They see the resource and expect a matching service. There is little that you can do about this perception except to be aware of it and do your best to respond accordingly. Remember that some employers would swap good fundamentals in perception by key target audiences for a good press. Your aim must be to achieve both.

In managing your media relations the first priority is availability. Contact numbers need to be known to the media and to provide a round-the-clock service. The members of your team who deal with the media must be well briefed on likely issues and hold position statements backed up by question-and-answer briefs.

All information provided to the media, either proactively or responsively, must be short, clear, factual and free from puffery. Remember the old maxim – who? what? how? when? where? why? Avoid jargon when you speak to the media and always visualise your words in print or on air. You and your management are never, ever off the record with journalists or anyone else other than your retained professional advisers and even then there are qualifications. If you assume that there is no such state of existence as off the record you will be the least likely to regret your words. Use media call sheets to record details of the contacts that have been handled.

Be well briefed

Be well informed and well briefed so that you are confident about what you may disclose, and you will be a good source for the media. If you cannot take a call, ring back immediately and assume that the matter is urgent until the journalist tells you that it is not. Good access to your management will ensure that you can clarify situations and get statements approved quickly. Sometimes the journalist will want and deserve a fresh quote from the chief executive, so ensure that you can make them available quickly when this is justified. When you cannot say anything, try to give a reason. Work hard to understand the various media outlets and individual journalists, their needs, attitudes, readership and generally where they are coming from.

PUBLIC RELATIONS COLLEAGUES

Your external public relations colleagues are among the most valuable contacts you can develop. You will be able to relate to them through shared interests in a town, region or sector, or by area of public relations specialisation. The best place to meet them can often be the Institute of Public Relations through its national events, regional groups and specialist groups. Its handbook is an invaluable source of information and contacts.

There will be times when issues are best handled on a cooperative basis within a town or an industry sector and knowing your colleagues will facilitate this process. You will often want partners, customers, suppliers and organisations with an interest in your activities to assist with a bilateral announcement. Knowing your opposite number will give you a flying start. If there is a problem between two organisations, then a channel open between the public relations managers will be of benefit. You might also be able to help your management by checking out the special interests of a customer chief executive.

NETWORKING ADDS VALUE

Do not underestimate the potential value to your organisation of the networking you do. Join the appropriate organisations and invest some time.

Keep good records of all your contacts in the key target audiences for your organisation and of your own personal contacts. Use databases to keep track of everyone.

Be available at all times to your own management and to your key contacts. Be prepared to give your own home telephone number to your internal colleagues, the media and to others who need it. This will not prevent you from dropping polite hints if this courtesy is being abused by calls which could just as easily have been dealt with during the working day.

Insist on having a high-quality mobile telephone at your employer's expense and make good use of it. Ensure that all your contacts know where to find you by providing business cards and contact book stickers with all the necessary information. Make sure that your staff understand your attitude to your own availability and give you the right support.

Possessing contacts and information and being rapidly available to share them are key factors for success in public relations and will add value to your own performance.

13

General administration

The most important subject of financial administration has already been covered in Chapter 6 and other aspects are covered throughout this book. This chapter deals with some other specific areas as well as the general principles.

A well-organised department with good systems of working will be far more cost effective and reliable than one which is disorganised. Systematic procedures will reduce errors dramatically and help to create a good impression of your operation both internally and externally.

INFORMATION TECHNOLOGY

Efficient utilisation of information technology (IT) will be one of the most important factors in the effective administration of your department.

Key factors in managing IT

- allocate a specific responsibility for IT
- develop skills across the team
- plan hardware needs in the capital process
- standardise on one software suite
- avoid customised databases if possible
- utilise internal and external networks
- avoid complex desktop publishing systems

Getting specialist help

The specification and application of computer software and hardware is a field in which you are likely to need specialist help. Nevertheless, you need to learn as much as possible from reading and courses so that you will understand what can be done.

Your own organisation may have a specialist IT team or may use an outside consultant. Unfortunately, the computer industry is full of technical buffs who are unable to explain the technology in everyday language. This has been a bar to the exploitation of new technology in many fields. Another problem is that your own in-house computing department may have specialised in applications related to the organisation's mainline business, be it engineering or medical records. They may have little empathy with your specialist functional requirements.

You are likely to be using a specialist agency to design or maintain your Web site. There are also one or two public relations consultancies which have specialised in the general application of IT in the public relations industry and are willing to sell their expertise. This can be a useful route because you are dealing with colleagues who understand your business.

Give priority to developing IT capability

You will want to develop IT skills right across your team and it needs to be given high priority in your overall departmental training plan. It is also a good idea to allocate to one member of your team a particular responsibility for developing and managing your departmental systems.

You must insist on having high-quality IT support for your programmes or you will not be competitive or efficient. You must make sure that you make any capital submissions you need in good time in order to obtain the hardware you require.

Identify your particular needs

It is not possible to give specific advice here as the technology is moving forward so rapidly, but there are some obvious starting points.

On the hardware front, your minimum requirements will include personal computers and printers together with modems for external linking. The capability of sending material direct to outside suppliers and target audiences is essential.

You will need access to the appropriate internal and external networks. You have to be able to access information, store and retrieve information and transmit it to others as necessary.

Managing text in a variety of ways is an obvious priority so you must specify state-of-the-art wordprocessing software within a general office system such as MicroSoft (MS) Word within MS Office. This will be used for generating customised news releases, speech writing, producing text for brochures and reports and myriad other activities which are routine in a busy public relations department. MS PowerPoint is an effective standard tool for creating presentations.

Use a standard database tool

You will need a first-class standard database tool for managing all your listings, from the special interests of parliamentary representatives to your magazine mailing lists. Ensure that you comply with all legal requirements covering data protection. There are simple low-cost standard database tools such as MS Access which will hold many fields of information with large numbers of entries and are able to produce a variety of standard reports, and search for and sort information. Sometimes these tools are unpopular with IT specialists who would rather sell you a costly customised tool for each individual application.

Design your database needs around the capability of your standard tool and ensure that your staff are as comfortable with it as with their wordprocessor software.

Introducing creativity

Most of the standard office software packages will give you a capability for dealing with budget administration, spreadsheets, pie charts, histograms and other illustrations.

You may also have a use for simple design and layout software which is readily available or may come as a standard element in your main software package. Think very carefully before you go beyond this into the more costly specialist design and desktop publishing systems. If your requirements are modest, it may be wiser to avoid the investment in hardware, software and highly trained staff and instead buy someone else's spare capacity.

Back-up

Whatever else you do, make sure that all the information is backed up regularly and held securely at another location as an insurance against fire, theft or technical failure. Your organisation may well have standard back-up systems. If not, perhaps you can exchange tapes in sealed bags weekly with a professional adviser or another department on a different site.

HARD COPY STORAGE AND RETRIEVAL

Clearly, you will make the maximum use of your electronic systems for information storage and retrieval. Nevertheless, there is still a value in maintaining hard copy files of some major items. For example, you will want security copies of all significant news releases, newsletters and magazines, reports and accounts, video programmes and other such strategic materials. These will naturally be stored in chronological order. It can be useful to maintain a computer database referencing coverage of major issues in all these items.

For example, if your organisation has sponsored a charity fun run, you could produce a listing showing the date of all reports of this in news releases, your own magazine and corporate brochures. You could also include the photo library location reference for the main pictures you hold. Such a database will make it so much easier for you to track issues and quickly assemble all the definitive information on a particular subject. It will take you quickly to the hard copy without you having to spend hours searching through the files.

Establish a clear retention policy

More generally, you will need to have a clear and written policy on what items need to be retained, for how long and in what format. Your organisation should have an overall policy on archiving with which you will be required to comply. This will cover such matters as retention of contractual and legal papers, financial and tax records and other such items. You will need to consult with your colleagues in other departments such as personnel and legal, particularly the manager who has overall responsibility for archiving policy.

In addition, you should make your own realistic assessment of which items originated by you need to be retained and for how long. In particular, it is important to keep all public statements indefinitely.

Historic archive

Apart from archiving for legal purposes, your organisation should maintain an archive for historic purposes. There may be a clear policy on this which places the responsibility on your own or some other department. In any event, there is satisfaction in ensuring that there is a good historic archive of the organisation during your period of stewardship.

The simplest way of tackling this is to store security copies at the year end of the annual report, the corporate magazine and any major brochures or videos produced during the year. You can add copies of significant news releases and a few of the most important pictures of the year together with other items which are appropriate to your particular role. Good-quality box files or safe boxes boldly labelled are one simple way of storing this material. There might be one or two for each year and they could save future generations a great deal of heartache when major anniversaries occur.

PICTURE LIBRARY

Your organisation may have a number of picture libraries or the ultimate responsibility for the library may lie with you. There are few facilities which can turn into a mess as quickly as a picture library which contains every shot ever taken, in different formats and stored in a hotchpotch of envelopes and folders.

Invest in a good-quality picture storage system and make sure that you are highly selective about which items will be stored in the long term. Those items which do not meet your criteria should be thrown away after a defined period or returned to the originator if this was another department. You may have to be tough if you wish to avoid being smothered under a mass of pictures of leaving presentations and long-service awards and out-of-date shots of your chairperson.

You should ensure that there is a good index system which enables material to be found easily. You will need a system which your entire team can follow rather than an approach which relies on the personal knowledge of one individual. There must be a good lending record system which shows who is holding all the pictures that are not currently in the library and when they were removed. This has to be reinforced by a follow-up system so that outstanding loans are chased and recovered.

Plan your picture library content

The content of the photo library should be planned in a proactive way. Draw up a matrix of the range of pictures which would cover the breadth of your organisation's activities, enabling you to meet basic media requests and support your own needs for brochures and other applications. Then try to plan opportunities to pick up pictures over a period to cover the elements of your matrix.

Typical extracts from photo library matrix

People
The founder.
Senior management.
Previous management.
Action shots of people in facilities.

Facilities
Corporate headquarters.
High-technology manufacturing.
UK facilities.
USA facilities.
Germany facilities.
Spain facilities.
Singapore service centre.
China joint venture.

Products and Services
Food products.
Dairy equipment division products.
Drinks products.
Franchise service centres.

Events
Employee consultation meetings.
Factory openings.
Signing of China joint venture.

MEDIA DISTRIBUTION AND MONITORING

Several services specialise in maintaining databases of media contacts and distributing news releases for in-house operations and consultancies. Unless your needs are limited and specialist, it will normally be most cost efficient for you to use these services rather than to replicate their systems within your department.

In the same way you are likely to use media monitoring services to collect references to your organisation in both print and broadcast media. Some services specialise in the more immediate coverage of the daily national press and wire services; others provide a similar service for broadcast media. These services can be expensive but are generally efficient and rarely miss references.

Services also exist which focus on collecting large quantities of cuttings from less immediate sources such as the regional press and specialist trade and technical publications. These services tend to give good value, although their coverage is not comprehensive and clips may take some time to reach you.

Circulating media coverage

Study of your coverage will provide valuable feedback for your media relations activity, indicating the interests of particular journalists and the type of stories which are used. Clippings should also be circulated to your colleagues around the organisation to give them the necessary information about what is being said. You should make sure that a digest of coverage is sent to your management board so that they have a balanced picture of it.

The use of media monitoring services should not prevent your team from following the media closely themselves so that they have a good working knowledge of the approach adopted and the special interests of the various journalists.

Many departments produce an 'intelligence service' for management covering media extracts which are of general interest such as supplier news and articles about competitors and shareholders. Bear in mind that some media owners expect copyright payments for the reproduction of their material within monitoring reports.

PROCEDURES AND QUALITY STANDARDS

A well-managed department will have carefully defined procedures for dealing with all the routine daily work. These should include the way the telephone is answered: the target maximum number of rings before pickup; the words used in response; and the way messages are taken, recorded, passed on and dealt with.

Procedures should also be established for processing faxes, handling post, receiving personal callers and managing all the other routines.

All these procedures should be incorporated in a departmental operating manual. This will provide a vehicle for ensuring uniform and high-standard performance of routine tasks. It will be an invaluable tool for new starters and for anyone working within the department on a temporary basis. Such a manual will take you a long way towards obtaining certification under one of the internationally recognised quality standards such as BS5750 or ISO 9000.

Typical contents of an office procedures manual

- contact lists
- general office procedures
- budget control procedures
- security of information
- responding to telephone calls
- handling mail and e-mail
- holidays, sickness and office cover
- filing systems
- information systems and databases, access and ownership
- monitoring and circulating media coverage
- dealing with media calls
- format and authority for media announcements
- house style for copy
- crisis communication procedure

14

Working with public relations consultancies

CONSULTANCY IS A DIFFERENT WORLD

Almost certainly you will have some work which is best assigned to external consultancies, and managing these relationships effectively could have a noticeable impact on the performance and cost of your department.

The public relations consultant uses the same techniques as the in-house practitioner but there are substantial environmental differences in the way they operate. Consultants have to worry about billable hours and timesheets and divide their time between the demands of a number of clients. They can get a buzz from working with professional colleagues on a wide variety of programmes. However, they can rarely have the sense of total single-minded involvement and commitment to one cause which you should have.

The senior in-house practitioner should have access to everything which is happening in the organisation and its future options. You cannot expect your consultancies to know your business better than you do and of course you are employing them for other reasons.

REASONS FOR EMPLOYING CONSULTANCIES

In planning your total departmental resource you will need to consider the variety of ways in which consultancy support could help you to deliver effective programmes on time and within budget.

Ten reasons for employing consultancies
- second opinion on strategy
- implementing programmes
- filling experience and capability gaps
- providing overseas resource
- special situations such as bids and listings
- access to contacts
- research
- meeting workload peaks
- supporting subsidiary operations
- reinforcing issues to management

Strategic support

You might want a consultancy to develop an overall communication strategy for your organisation but, if so, you must question whether you are in the right job. Nobody is in a better position to define the strategy than you are, working with your own team and your manager. However, it can be useful to obtain a second opinion on your strategy from consultants who understand your target audiences. This is not necessarily the 'detached view' referred to by some consultants who claim that this is a vital requirement in public relations work which only they can provide. The fact is that you must remain detached and unemotional about the issues your employer faces if you are to be effective. Few public relations consultants employ other consultancies to give them a detached view of their own public relations programmes, which rather tends to weaken that argument.

Implementation support

You might decide to employ consultancies to implement all or most of the strategies you have developed in house. Some organisations which are keen on outsourcing and maintaining a low headcount favour this approach. It is unlikely to result in cost savings, however, as an efficient in-house department should be at least as well managed and cost effective as the leading consultancies.

Using consultants to fill specific experience and capability gaps in your own department can provide the most productive balance between internal and external resource. For example, you might have a basic requirement for government relations services but one not large enough to justify the employment of an internal specialist. A modest retainer to a public affairs specialist should meet your needs. It could be that you need support in one or two international markets but on a scale which does not justify setting up an in-house department there. Here again consultancy can get you up and running quickly, and cost effectively.

Bids and listings

Most major public companies now carry out their routine financial communication work in house. Often this is supplemented by the use of a financial communication or investor relations specialist consultancy. Few in-house practitioners will gain enough experience of special financial situations such as bids or listings to be totally confident in being up to date with best practice in these areas. It is a natural area for calling in support from a consultancy which is handling a variety of such activities for clients on a regular basis.

Access to contacts and research

Gaining access to contacts is another justification for utilising consultancy. There may be marginal areas of activity where you do not have sufficient involvement to build up your own network of contacts. Your occasional requirements for access can be satisfied by utilising a consultancy which has regular work in that field and thus has developed its own contact base.

The better public relations consultancies will contain practitioners with broad knowledge and experience, particularly if they have a wide client base. Such companies can be a valuable source of background briefings, perhaps to support new ventures or your chairperson's overseas visits. If you need some *ad hoc* background research carried out you should consider the possibility of placing the job with a public relations consultancy which is likely to have all the skills needed for such tasks.

When workload exceeds capacity

The most obvious reason for using a consultancy is when the sheer volume of work to be completed in a specific period exceeds your capacity. This might be because of vacancies in your team or some unexpected development. In some organisations there are occasional natural peaks in workload. A busy department is more likely to be effective than one which is overstaffed, apart from financial considerations. There can be sense in staffing for the normal level of work and dealing with the peaks by buying surplus capacity from a consultant.

'Stand-by' retainers

Some organisations pay retainers to consultants just to keep them briefed and available to meet an emergency or planned future development. There are limited circumstances in which this can be justified, but this should not provide a rationale for a substantial fee. After all, the consultancy is automatically plugged into a possible future new business opportunity in exchange for some elementary monitoring. Unfortunately, faced with this situation, some consultants insist on a high retainer and then look for work to justify this. It is worth bearing in mind that if there is a hostile bid for your company you will receive immediate offers of help from leaders in that field while your standby consultant might be prevented from acting by their existing commercial relationships or antipathy from your broker or merchant bank.

Outsourcing subsidiary needs

Even if your own need for consultancy services is limited, outsourcing may be the best way of supporting your overseas, regional or subsidiary operations. If their needs are limited it can be difficult to recruit or to justify the cost of high-quality in-house staff. This is a logical time to use a consultancy but make sure that you are the person making or approving the selection and exerting a major influence over the activity.

Just occasionally you might want to use a consultancy to reinforce your own views with your management or even to get an issue on to the agenda from an outside source. If you are a successful practitioner, with the confidence of your management, this should be a rare eventuality but it is worth considering in special circumstances.

ETHICAL AND PROFESSIONAL STANDARDS

You will want to ensure that your chosen consultancy will operate to a code of ethical conduct and to high professional standards. In the area of general public relations, the Public Relations Consultants Association (PRCA) provides a basis for professional consultancy practice in the United Kingdom.

Member firms of the PRCA have to meet an externally assessed standard to confirm that they are managed on a commercially competent basis. In addition, they are bound by a code of ethical standards concerning their conduct towards clients and both internal and external audiences. The PRCA provides a complaints arbitration service, which can order the ultimate penalty of expulsion from the organisation. There is also a standard PRCA contract which can be used and is endorsed by the IPR.

Some excellent consultancies are not members of the PRCA, but should still be able to provide you with information about their ethical approach. They may be members of other industry bodies that have codes or may have adopted their own individual codes of practice. In either case, your position is clearer if the practitioners who work on your account are individual members of the IPR and are also subject to its professional code.

SELECTING AND APPOINTING CONSULTANCIES

You and your chosen consultants will need to invest money, time and effort to get the best from the relationship. It is well worth putting considerable effort into making the right appointment in the first place.

Key steps in selecting a consultancy
- identify your essential needs
- produce a long list of candidates
- invite credentials-only presentations
- choose a short list
- now provide a detailed brief
- compare final presentations
- appoint and agree remuneration

Analysing the options available

Types of consultancy
- wholly owned international groups
- large independent operations
- international networks of independents
- smaller, more specialist businesses
- independent practitioners and associates

You can select a consultant from an extremely wide variety of companies, some of which are large international groups employing many hundreds of consultants around the world. Other companies are based in one country but have operating links to other independent businesses overseas. Some excellent small operations exist which employ a handful of people and there are highly capable individuals who have chosen to work alone for a small number of clients.

Independent consultants can cover a wide range of capabilities from strategic advice on integrated communication to implementation support. Some specialise in particular areas such as financial or marketing communication, while others specialise in particular technical skills such as writing or events management.

You must consider your needs and the type of operation which is most likely to fulfil them, but do keep your mind and your options open in the early stages of your search.

There are several ways of managing an international programme. In our shrinking world most consultancies now offer an international capability. If you have the time, it could be worthwhile to select the most appropriate consultant in each country where the programme will be implemented. However, this is time consuming and you will also have to continue to provide individual briefing and performance monitoring in each market. An international group or network will look after the international management and co-ordination for you. On the other hand, they are unlikely to have the best operation for your needs in each and every country.

If your programme covers a wide range of audiences you will need to consider whether you should employ several specialist consultancies to cover the sectors such as financial communication and government relations. Alternatively, you might use one supplier which has a broad capability but is not necessarily the most effective in each area.

If your project only needs a minimal amount of consultancy time, you can get very good value for money from using independent practitioners. They are likely to have lower overheads and lower hourly rates than companies and obviously you will get personal attention. It is important to be sure that they can be available when you need them as they may have little back-up.

Identifying the long list of candidate consultancies

Often there is no right or wrong way to resource your consultancy needs. You have many options and much will depend on how the consultants perform during the appointment process.

The first step is to agree the essentials within your own team: whether you need particular sector experience or language capability; which competing client accounts would be a bar to appointment; and all the other factors which you consider to be essential.

The next stage is to produce a long list of operations which appear to meet your criteria. This might include five to a dozen or so companies. In identifying this list you will, of course, include consultancies you know personally or which have been recommended to you by trusted contacts. In the UK the Public Relations

Consultants Association (PRCA) produces a useful handbook of its members. However, there are some excellent companies which have chosen not to join the PRCA which you can find on the ranking lists produced by *PR Week*.

Register services offer the ability to review agency presentations on paper and video, in one central location and without the consultancies knowing of your interest. The IPR is a superb source of contacts for individual consultants and you should study its handbook and utilise its 'Matchmaker' skills database.

Initial credentials presentations

Having created your long list, you should then visit their offices and ask for a credentials presentation. You may be asked to provide a brief, but this is too early a stage to do this. let the consultancies tell you about themselves without being influenced by knowledge of your specific needs. If you do provide a brief at this point, there is a danger that the consultants will slant their credentials presentation to emphasise their experience in your area and this can have a distorting effect on your appraisal.

Some issues to clarify in the presentations

- ownership of the consultancy
- client base
- relevant or conflicting accounts
- relevant experience
- consultancy commitment to professional development
- who will actually work on the account and to what extent
- experience of the account team
- how the consultancy will report on the programme
- frequency of internal and joint account reviews
- budget monitoring and reporting procedures
- hourly rates of consultants
- is there an hourly fee for the administration team?
- method of charging for post, fax, copying, travel, etc
- mark-up placed on external costs
- how performance will be evaluated jointly
- will the consultancy assign copyright to the client when possible?

The final short list

Following these visits you can produce a short list of consultants who you want to bid for the business. Typically, this might include between three and five names. This is the point at which you provide an initial brief which defines your needs. It should include: general background on your organisation; an outline of your overall public relations strategies and programmes; the objective of the consultancy role; your budget; and all the other information relevant to the appointment.

The final presentations

In order to maintain a consistent appraisal, the consultancies should each present to the same team, which should include your management if they are going to take an active part in the decision. It is better if all the presentations can take place on the same day or on consecutive days.

The decision-making process should be well structured. List the criteria which are important to you and design scoring sheets to be used by your team (see Table 14.1). These will include such matters as: understanding of and response to your brief; the quality of the account team as distinct from the presentation team; cost; size; location; creativity of the approach adopted; and all the other factors you consider important. Do not ignore that instinct in these matters which some people call 'chemistry'.

Table 14.1 *Sample score sheet for presentations*

	Score
Overall quality of response to the brief	30
Creativity of approach	10
Budget	10
Quality of account team versus presentation team	20
Account handling issues such as location	10
Comfort with them to represent the organisation	20
	100

FORMALISING THE APPOINTMENT

When you have made your selection you will need to agree contractual terms. If this is an *ad hoc* project assignment, it should be a straightforward matter with an agreed cost and a defined duration. Longer relationships need more careful thought. There is nothing worse than being tied to a long contract when one party is dissatisfied with the relationship. Bearing in mind that the consultancy will need time to establish the programme and produce results, you should consider giving an initial six months' security of tenure with either party able to terminate the relationship with three months' notice after the first six months.

Methods of payment

You can remunerate your consultancy in several ways. The easiest from the client's point of view is a fixed retainer for an agreed programme. Consultants will often prefer a 'time input' relationship which allows them to bill you for the actual hours worked. This can produce budgetary shocks for you if the situation is not carefully managed. There are also intermediate systems in which a target retainer is agreed based on an estimated number of hours to carry out the programme. Under these systems you might discuss credits if fewer hours are worked or additional charges if extra hours are worked. Hours actually worked need to be flagged up regularly.

In the end, all consultancy charges will have to relate one way or another to the hours worked by their employees for that is what they are selling. Make sure that you agree how out-of-pocket expenses are authorised and billed and whether items disbursed are marked up and at what rate. This area can be damaging to relationships if the position is not clearly defined and agreed.

MAKING THE RELATIONSHIP WORK

The main ingredients, apart from performance, for a successful relationship will be mutual confidence and communication. Good and regular programme reporting and contact reporting are needed from the consultant to you and regular briefing is needed from you to the consultant.

Always give feedback on how you and your organisation view performance and do not allow the relationship to deteriorate in small stages but deal with issues as they arise. Your consultants are an extension of your own team and you should treat them accordingly if you want to obtain value for money.

15

Managing your own career

DIFFERING ASPIRATIONS

When managing your department in the best interests of your organisation, you should not neglect to manage your own career in *your own* best interests. If you do this professionally, it will also benefit your current employer for as long as you can continue to find job satisfaction within your present organisation.

We are all different and have different aspirations for our working lives. For some, it is primarily a method of acquiring the maximum wealth while others seek the personal satisfaction of making a significant contribution to a worthwhile cause whilst accepting a modest personal standard of material wealth. Some wish to test their abilities to the limit of their potential while others are happier performing at a level that they can comfortably achieve.

In any case, personal career management needs to be given attention. You may think that you have the most interesting and rewarding job you could wish to have, but be aware that the pace of change may catch you out. Your current role could disappear as a result of a business merger or acquisition. New technology or a change in legislation could affect your employer's requirements for your services. At a more personal level, you might have to work with a new senior manager with whom your approach is not compatible. This is a particular hazard in the public relations discipline where you have to give detached and sometimes personal advice to your senior management.

The advice in this chapter is aimed at helping ambitious practitioners to develop their careers, but much of it should be followed even if you are contented so that you will be prepared for any future changes to your situation.

WHEN SHOULD YOU CHANGE YOUR JOB?

If you join a large or growing successful organisation, you might just spend all or most of your career there, even if you are ambitious. Instead of moving on, your role could develop so that you become the head of the communication function and then move on into general management.

If you have completed a formal academic qualification in public relations, you should aim to stay in your first job for at least two years. This is normally the minimum time needed to learn about the sector, gain practical experience and notch up some real achievements. Of course, this may not apply if you really do hate the job after a reasonable period or if you get offered a new opportunity that is too good to refuse. Generally, though, a stable start to your career will look attractive to future employers and recruitment agencies.

When you accept your first job, there is some benefit to having your second job in mind. This will enable you to take a balanced view about aspects of the first role that may not match your immediate aspirations, but will set you up well for the future. For example, you might join an organisation that does not set the pace for salary levels but is well known for the quality of its training and development policies. Therefore, you might view your first two target jobs as a single package.

Some people believe that three years in a role can be about right. In this theory, the first year is about learning and experimenting, the second year is one of successful implementation and in the third year performance is polished and achievement peaks. Of course, this would not necessarily lead on to a job change but to an extension of role and responsibility. There are no hard and fast rules because many organisations now have to change rapidly to adapt to external forces. Certainly, anyone who changed employers every third year throughout their career could be viewed with caution by recruiters.

A SPELL IN CONSULTANCY?

If you are an in-house practitioner, there are real benefits to spending some time in a senior role in consultancy. It will give you an opportunity to work more closely with other specialists in your field, whilst at the same time gaining exposure to a variety of sectors and the different organisational cultures of your client base. You will also learn much about the ways in which consultancies operate, which will help you to get the best value from working with them as a client in the future.

It may be better to seize such an opportunity when it arises rather than pursue it too determinedly at the risk of interrupting natural progression in-house. The experience will only be of real career value if you join a consultancy that is an overall leader or a leader within a specialist field which is of interest to you. The quality of the client base with which you will be working is another vital factor. It could provide you with an attractive route back in-house. Alternatively, you may find consultancy life so attractive that you stay on and develop your career in this area!

BEYOND PUBLIC RELATIONS

You may have the ambition and the ability to progress from a leading role in public relations into general management. In the past, the function was not necessarily seen as a natural step for such progression. This is now changing as organisations recognise the significance of reputation and communication, and at the same time the quality of the people in our function continues to advance rapidly.

If your role is corporate, you will have a much better overall understanding of your organisation than most of your colleagues. In order to progress beyond your current function, you need to add many other qualities to this useful base.

You will need to ensure that you are selected for your employer's general management development programmes – whether these are internal or external. If this does not happen, you should make arrangements in your own time and at your own expense. In particular, you must acquire financial skills. You must be able to understand and analyse a profit-and-loss account and a balance sheet, together with related financial reports. It is crucial that these financial capabilities are fully developed if you are working in the business sector.

You should also aim to earn a place on the various working groups, committees and boards, where you will sit alongside other functional specialists and general managers. In these bodies, you will be able to ensure that communication plays a full role in the organisation, learn a great deal by observation and begin to make a name for yourself by the contribution you make.

THE VALUE OF MENTORS

If you have ability, you are likely to find that a number of people will take an interest in your career. It will be very helpful to have a handful of such people, whose knowledge and judgement you respect, who can act informally as your mentors. Often, they will be older than you and have a broad experience and range of contacts.

Your mentors will be able to give you a second opinion about opportunities you are considering and advise you at times when you feel that your career is not moving forward as you wish. They can also serve as referees when needed. If you find yourself in a tricky situation, they will be there in the background to provide support.

People who fulfil this role most effectively do it because they themselves have benefited from similar relationships in their own careers. They may well be most valuable if they are uninvolved in your immediate personal or working situations and therefore able to give detached advice when needed. Such relationships develop best spontaneously and informally and may last for much of your career.

A HIGH-QUALITY CV IS VITAL

Think of your CV as the equivalent of your corporate brochure, report and accounts, sales brochure and new business tender. The general quality of CV presentation has improved significantly in recent times, but there are still too many sloppy documents on offer.

Essential contents of one-page summary CV

- comprehensive contact information
- brief description and statement of aims
- relevant educational and professional qualifications
- nationality or clarification of employment eligibility
- age
- brief career summary – positions, employers and dates, with any gaps explained
- brief statement of relevant achievements and capability for position sought

You should aim to set out your summary CV on one page. It needs to work as a stand-alone document, as it may become separated from your accompanying letter. You can offer or attach an extended version that gives additional information, including more details of your responsibilities and your important achievements in previous jobs. Your standard CV should be amended to include any information that has been specifically requested by a researcher or in an advertisement. You can also use a one-page covering letter to reinforce some key points.

A short description and 'mission statement' should appear boldly in a prominent position. This should be no more than one or two brief sentences such as, 'A public relations graduate with a successful track record in financial communication now ready for a wider corporate role in a major company'.

It seems too obvious to say that there should be no typographical errors, but the proportion of such mistakes in a typical sample is surprising. A careless attitude to such an important personal document can be taken as indicative of a general shortfall in attention to detail. Recruitment consultants are usually very interested in any chronological gaps in a CV, so these need careful explanation. Some candidates cause confusion by displaying work experience attachments or vacation work in the same way as actual career positions. Unless these are highly relevant to the position sought, they rarely deserve more than a passing reference. Depending on your career structure, it may be necessary to comment on why you made a particular change that may not look logical unless explained.

RECRUITMENT AGENCIES AND HEADHUNTERS

A large proportion of the senior jobs in public relations are filled with the support of outside agencies. There is a wide variety of these agencies, but their activities and involvement can be summarised in three major categories.

At the lower level of appointment, there are agencies that maintain large databases of candidates and place recruitment advertising for companies. Much of their work is for consultancies. If you register with agencies at this level for the first time, you might find yourself offered to a large number of potential employers – particularly those consultancies that are always on the lookout for new talent. This can be frustrating as there may have been only a limited amount of effort applied to matching your aims with those of potential employers.

The next level consists of recruitment search consultancies that have chosen to specialise in the communication sector and perform a true headhunting service for clients. These organisations maintain more senior databases and, because of their specialisation, are extremely well informed about the public relations industry, its leaders and the future talent pool. They are used by many employers to fill middle- and senior-management roles in public relations. It is important to be on these consultancy databases. At the right time in your career development, you should write to them with your short CV, your extended version and a brief explanation of your current career aims. It is likely that you will initially be invited to a meeting with a researcher. If this does not happen, telephone a researcher to seek such a meeting.

Sometimes, the most senior appointments in public relations are filled using the support of international executive search consultants that do not have a functional specialisation. These firms have a minimum salary level below which they will not become involved, except in special circumstances. Large companies may have a long-term relationship with a particular headhunter who deals with all their director-level requirements. Some of these consultancies have relevant experience in public relations recruitment, but others have limited experience of handling these appointments. When you have reached a senior level, you should write to these headhunters in the same way as you would to public relations specialists. You will almost certainly receive a polite reply that will make it obvious to you whether your current level of achievement is yet on their 'radar screen'.

Once you are making a name for yourself, actively networking and well regarded by your peer group, you will receive calls from headhunters, whether or not you are already on their databases. This will be because other senior practitioners have mentioned your name or because potential employers have noticed the results of your work. If the job under discussion is not of interest to you, you may be asked whether you can suggest anyone else who might be appropriate. In fact, the initial question may well have been put on the basis of, 'do you know anyone...' when the headhunter is not yet ready or able to focus on you as a target. In order to maintain your own credibility, it is important that you only suggest alternative candidates with whom you would be prepared to work yourself.

An initial approach from a headhunter can be the start of a very long process involving exchanging your latest CV for a job profile, followed by an interview with the recruiter, psychometric analysis and a series of meetings with the potential employer.

ETHICAL ASPECTS OF PUBLIC RELATIONS MANAGEMENT

Your employers have a right to expect a high standard of professional competence and performance from you. They are equally entitled to expect you to operate within a proper ethical framework. You also owe it to yourself to manage your own reputation as effectively as you manage that of the organisation you represent.

YOUR ORGANISATION'S ETHICAL CODES

It is almost certain that your employer will have well-defined ethical codes. These will be influenced by the nature of its activities and the organisations with which it has to deal. If these codes are inadequately recorded or publicised internally, it is appropriate for you to recommend action to redress this.

Internal codes of ethical conduct may be contained within individual employee contracts or on a separate addendum attached to these. They might also be presented as a statement within the company's report and accounts, in other literature, on the Web site or be displayed within premises.

Wide awareness of these codes helps to enhance your corporate reputation and to ensure consistent behaviour by all employees. It is also helpful in defending the organisation's position if it has to deal with the consequences of unethical behaviour by individual employees.

YOUR OWN PROFESSIONAL CODE

One of the most significant benefits of joining the Institute of Public Relations is the code of conduct, which is binding on all members. It covers such issues as professional integrity, personal conduct, adherence to the codes of other bodies, competence, conflicts of interest, confidentiality and the maintenance of professional standards. The Institute provides guidance notes on interpretation of the code and enforces it through professional practices review and disciplinary systems. Practitioners who are concerned about ethical issues are able to obtain informal advice from senior colleagues.

Those of your colleagues in other functions who are also members of their own professional bodies will also be bound by their codes of conduct. It is worthwhile ensuring that your management is aware that the practice of public relations has its own ethical parameters in the same way as accountancy and human resources management.

ETHICAL STANDARDS OF OTHER ORGANISATIONS

You must ensure that you are aware of the rules and ethical codes of the various organisations with which you have an involvement. These include the rules governing the way in which you influence elected representatives and public officials. In a corporate role, the rules governing the public listing of your company's shares will be of enormous importance in the way you manage communication for the business. Marketing communication is also subject to rigorous control in many areas, from advertising standards to specific product area requirements such as those concerning the medical sector.

It is essential that you and your team work closely within the legal, regulatory and ethical framework within each country in which you practise public relations. You should carry out a regular audit of your own awareness in these areas and ensure that you have systems in place to keep you up to date with changes in practice.

You will need to ensure that your suppliers and representatives adhere to ethical codes and are aware of those that you have adopted. This is most important when working with consultants who may be directly representing your own opinions to others. It will be helpful to you in managing this issue if they are members of a trade association with a code of conduct such as the Public Relations Consultants Association in the United Kingdom.

DEALING WITH AN ETHICAL PROBLEM

If you believe that something that your employer is asking you to do is unethical, there are various steps you can take. First, you should attempt to resolve the situation with your immediate manager. If this fails, you should ask for a discussion at a higher level of management. While this is in process, you might seek confidential advice at a senior level within the IPR if you believe you are being asked to breach your own professional ethical code. Alternatively, you could suggest that advice be taken by your employer from any other body that may be an obvious arbiter on the issue.

In the vast majority of cases, these actions will result in a satis-factory resolution of the dilemma. In some instances, there might be a temporary solution by which you are excused any personal involvement in the particular action while everyone takes time to give further consideration to the position. It is important to main-tain discussion and seek help rather than back yourself or your employer into an irretrievable position.

Of course, we are assuming here that you are not being asked to break the law or condone an action that is clearly unacceptable. We are also assuming that the matter concerns a formal professional code of conduct rather than your own personal view. For example, if you would personally be unwilling to promote armaments or tobacco, you are unlikely to take a job with a manufacturer of such products. Such personal preferences may cause more difficulty for consultants, who may be best advised to raise them with employers at the time of appointment.

Appendix

PUBLIC RELATIONS EDUCATION AND TRAINING MATRIX

This document was established to set out the broad range of knowledge and skills necessary for a public relations professional. It was developed with and endorsed by the PRCA and the IPR. It forms an introduction to the subject – more detailed information can be found on the IPR Web site (www.ipr.org.uk). The matrix provides a platform for:

- self-assessment of training needs and career development;
- appraisal of employees' skills and their development needs;
- evaluation of training and education course suitability.

The matrix

The matrix is in four categories:

A: Knowledge.
B: Business skills.
C: Public relations skills – counsel and planning.
D: Public relations skills – implementation.

Five stages of knowledge, skills or experience have been identified:

Stage 1 – pre-entry requirements basic skills and knowledge necessary for any candidate wishing to pursue a career in public relations – these may be developed while working in an administrative role.

Stage 2 – professional starter – specific initial knowledge and skills essential for those developing their public relations career, from assistants and junior executives.

Stage 3 – developing and operating professional – development, **and 4** knowledge and skills, necessarily gained over a period of time, to become a fully rounded and experienced public relations practitioner.

Stage 5 – experienced professional specialist and manager – the continuing development phase from functional to team or group supervision responsibility, senior counselling and management.

A		KNOWLEDGE STAGE:	1	2	3	4	5
	1	The role of Public Relations, both in-house and consultancy, in commercial and public sector organisation	✓	✓	✓	✓	✓
	2	An appreciation of the range of techniques and media available to public relations practitioners in the UK	✓	✓	✓	✓	✓
	3	The role, responsibilities, vocabulary, techniques, ethics, law and regulations relating to: – public relations	✓	✓	✓	✓	✓
		– marketing, advertising, research and behavioural studies, sales promotion, direct marketing, direct selling		✓	✓	✓	✓
	4	The role, responsibilities, vocabulary, techniques, ethics, law and regulations relating to: – print and broadcast media, publishing, telecommunications		✓	✓	✓	✓
		sponsorship		✓	✓	✓	✓
	5	The structure, priorities, distribution, basic economics, organisation and operation of: – manufacturing industry		✓	✓	✓	✓
		– service industries		✓	✓	✓	✓
		– financial institutions		✓	✓	✓	✓
		– central and local government		✓	✓	✓	✓
		– the public sector		✓	✓	✓	✓
		– voluntary organisations		✓	✓	✓	✓
		– membership bodies		✓	✓	✓	✓
		– the professions		✓	✓	✓	✓
	6	The legal, legislative and regulatory framework of the UK and the EU				✓	✓
	7	Organisational strategy and policy making, both concept and practice			✓	✓	✓
	8	Communication theory and practice		✓	✓	✓	✓
	9	Organisational: planning and management – missions/objectives			✓	✓	✓
		– culture and ethics		✓	✓	✓	✓
		– growth strategies				✓	✓
		– financial planning and sourcing				✓	✓
		– decision-making				✓	✓
		– change management				✓	✓
		– structural options		✓	✓	✓	✓
		– performance measurement			✓	✓	✓
		– stakeholder theory and power		✓	✓	✓	✓

B		BUSINESS SKILLS STAGE:	1	2	3	4	5
	1	Communications: Telephone technique	✓	✓	✓	✓	✓
	2	Meeting technique	✓	✓	✓	✓	✓
	3	Presentation technique		✓	✓	✓	✓
	4	Working as part of a team	✓	✓	✓	✓	✓
	5	Working as part of an organisation		✓	✓	✓	✓
	6	Networking (clients, colleagues, contacts)		✓	✓	✓	✓
	7	Induction and orientation				✓	✓
	8	Negotiating skills		✓	✓	✓	✓
	9	Organisational: Work flow planning and setting priorities	✓	✓	✓	✓	✓
	10	Interviewing and staff selection				✓	✓

151

B		BUSINESS SKILLS STAGE:	1	2	3	4	5
	11	Time management	✓	✓	✓	✓	
	12	Delegation and supervision	✓	✓	✓	✓	
	13	Motivation and leadership			✓	✓	✓
	14	Budget setting and control			✓	✓	✓
	15	Team building and management				✓	✓
	16	Training and development of individuals and teams				✓	✓
	17	Understanding and design of financial controls				✓	✓
	18	Understanding/design of quality controls, including ISO9000				✓	✓
	19	Human resource planning and management				✓	✓
	20	Analytical: Analysing annual reports and financial data			✓	✓	✓
	21	Understanding the use of research data			✓	✓	✓
	22	Desk research		✓	✓	✓	✓
	23	Communication audits			✓	✓	✓
	24	Risk analysis			✓	✓	✓
	25	Activity and resource analysis				✓	✓
	26	SWOT analysis				✓	✓

C		PUBLIC RELATIONS SKILLS – COUNSEL AND PLANNING STAGE:	1	2	3	4	5
	1	Understanding Public Relations objectives and strategies		✓	✓	✓	✓
	2	Identifying publics		✓	✓	✓	✓
	3	Understanding the differing emphasis of various market sectors, such as: – consumer, technical, financial, health and science			✓	✓	✓
	4	Formulating Public Relations objectives			✓	✓	✓
	5	Developing Public Relations strategies, both overall and contingency			✓	✓	✓
	6	Creating Public Relations plans for action			✓	✓	✓
	7	Monitoring and evaluating progress and delivery			✓	✓	✓
	8	Assessing Public Relations implications of general management plans and decisions				✓	✓
	9	Identifying trends, risks and issues relevant to an organisation			✓	✓	✓
	10	Assessing the Public Relations implications for an organisation of the plans and decisions of other organisations, including: – its market place – local and national government – the European community – national and international regulatory bodies – the media – special interest groups – the local community			✓ ✓ ✓ ✓ ✓ ✓ ✓	✓ ✓ ✓ ✓ ✓ ✓ ✓	✓ ✓ ✓ ✓ ✓ ✓ ✓
	11	Understanding the implications of international developments in the media			✓	✓	✓
	12	Counselling and advisory techniques				✓	✓
	13	Issue management				✓	✓
	14	Crisis management				✓	✓

D		PUBLIC RELATIONS SKILLS – IMPLEMENTATION STAGE:	1	2	3	4	5
	1	Business Writing: – agendas, meeting notes, memoranda, letters – reports, proposals, planning, progress	✓	✓ ✓	✓ ✓	✓ ✓	✓ ✓
	2	Editorial Writing: – photocalls, media alerts, photo captions, draft releases – briefing and feature material, news letters, proof reading – script development and writing	✓	✓ ✓	✓ ✓ ✓	✓ ✓ ✓	✓ ✓ ✓
	3	Speeches and Presentations			✓	✓	✓
	4	Selecting media to reach identified publics		✓	✓	✓	✓
	5	Compiling contact lists	✓	✓	✓	✓	✓
	6	Media liaison techniques and operation			✓	✓	✓
	7	Editorial planning and monitoring			✓	✓	✓
	8	Editorial promotions (competitions, reader offers)			✓	✓	✓
	9	Negotiating editorial features and interviews			✓	✓	✓
	10	Handling editorial enquiries		✓	✓	✓	✓
	11	Selecting external resources: photographer, designers, printers and researchers			✓	✓	✓
	12	The basics of photography		✓	✓	✓	✓
	13	Briefing a photographer			✓	✓	✓
	14	Event planning and management			✓	✓	✓
	15	Exhibition planning and management			✓	✓	✓
	16	Sponsorship selection, planning and organisation			✓	✓	✓
	17	Briefing designers			✓	✓	✓
	18	Print selection, briefing and production management			✓	✓	✓
	19	Capabilities of desktop publishing			✓	✓	✓
	20	Audio/visual briefing and production management			✓	✓	✓
	21	VNR/B-Roll production and distribution			✓	✓	✓
	22	Radio production and placement			✓	✓	✓
	23	Public speaking				✓	✓
	24	Giving interviews				✓	✓
	25	Conference and seminar participation				✓	✓

Index

Italics indicate tables or figures.

Visit Kogan Page on-line

Comprehensive information on
Kogan Page titles

Features include

- complete catalogue listings,
  including book reviews and
  descriptions

- special monthly promotions

- information on NEW titles and
  BESTSELLING titles

- a secure shopping basket facility
  for on-line ordering

PLUS everything you need to know
about KOGAN PAGE

http://www.kogan-page.co.uk